IS
MAGA
A TERRORIST MOVEMENT?

RUSSELL K. JACK
US Senior Federal Air Marshal, Retired

Is MAGA a Terrorist Movement?
Published by Horizon View Press LLC.
Denver, CO

Copyright ©2024 by Russell Jack. All rights reserved.

All rights reserved, including the right to reproduce any of this book, in part or in whole, in any form whatsoever, without the express written permission of the author. For information on permissions, or to contact the author, visit magaterrorism.com or email directly to russell@magaterrorism.com.

This work depicts actual events in the life of the author as truthfully as recollection permits. While all persons within are actual individuals, some names and identifying characteristics have been changed or omitted to respect their privacy. All author commentary, or opinions, in this book are just the author's opinions. The author does not encourage, imply, or support, any form of illegal activity; to include but not limited to; intimidation, coercion, harm, or terrorism.

No part of this book may be reproduced in any form or by any mechanical means, including information storage and retrieval systems without permission in writing from the publisher/author, except by a reviewer who may quote passages in a review.

All images, logos, quotes, and trademarks included in this book are subject to use according to trademark and copyright laws of the United States of America.

ISBN: 979-8-9900568-0-0
POLITICAL SCIENCE / Political Process / Campaigns & Elections

Cover and interior design by Victoria Wolf, wolfdesignandmarketing.com, copyright owned by Russell Jack.

QUANTITY PURCHASES: Schools, companies, professional groups, clubs, and other organizations may qualify for special terms when ordering quantities of this title. For information, email russell@magaterrorism.com.

All rights reserved by Russell Jack and Horizon View Press LLC.
Printed in the United States of America.

I dedicate this book to everyone in America who holds
our liberal democracy and our Constitution sacred.

America is what it is today because, even when we don't agree on
things, we find peaceful ways to work together and coexist. Our
people should not have to tolerate criminal and terrorist acts.
And those sworn to protect should ensure that this is the case.

It takes bravery to speak the truth and to
act and vote against tyranny.

Your actions and votes mean more now than ever.

Thank you for helping keep America the Land of the Free.

CONTENTS

Disclaimer vii

Preface 1

CHAPTER ONE
Introduction 5

CHAPTER TWO
But I *Am* MAGA 9

CHAPTER THREE
Identifying and Fixing the Problem 15

CHAPTER FOUR
Pseudo-Patriotism 19

CHAPTER FIVE
America, Land of the Free 27

CHAPTER SIX
OK, Now What? 37

CHAPTER SEVEN
Oath of Office 39

CHAPTER EIGHT
Terrorism vs. Tribalism 53

CHAPTER NINE
MAGA Terrorism 59

CHAPTER TEN
Government In Action 67

CHAPTER ELEVEN

MAGA in the House 73

CHAPTER TWELVE
Morality Police 79

CHAPTER THIRTEEN
Fascism 85

CHAPTER FOURTEEN
Fact vs. Fiction 87

CHAPTER FIFTEEN
GOP: The Party of Law and Order 95

CHAPTER SIXTEEN
The End Justifies the Means 97

CHAPTER SEVENTEEN
Is Trump a Traitor? 101

CHAPTER EIGHTEEN
Cult of Personality 109

CHAPTER NINETEEN
LGBTQ+ 113

CHAPTER TWENTY
Debunking MAGA 119

CHAPTER TWENTY-ONE
Freedom Under MAGA Rule 123

CHAPTER TWENTY-TWO
End Game 129

Notes 137

Gratitude 165

About the Author 167

DISCLAIMER

I AM SUPPOSED TO SAY "allegedly" anytime I refer to someone who has not been convicted of a crime. So, let's just assume that every time—of which there will be many—I allude to Trump, or anyone else who is charged or suspected of criminal wrongdoing, that they are "innocent until proven guilty in a court of law."

Although this book is based on fact supported by publicly available sources, I use my own experiences and interpretations as well. If you disagree with anything I say in this book, you are encouraged to check my sources and seek the truth. Feel free to find more information from other fact-checked and truthful sources as well. Not from right-wing "news" stations, but from other sources that don't revel in lying to you, over and over.

I know that I will be attacked, have my sources questioned, and everything else that is part of the MAGA doctrine. Why? Because that is what terrorists do. They want your silence, and for you to be scared and intimidated into their way of thinking, or at least not stopping them.

I started my journey as an agent primarily because of the terror attack against America on 9/11. They killed over 3,000 people, but they terrorized millions.

Do not give in! If you are for a truly free America, then keep up the fight! Take action (legally!), say something when it matters, and vote!

If you are a MAGA supporter, please be open to learning the facts. They do not match your worldview on patriotism. In fact, MAGA's actions are irrefutably *un*-American.

This is a fight for what is constitutional, legal, and right. If even one person can be convinced of the error of being part of the MAGA movement, or one person can fight harder to defend the Constitution and our modern American way of life, or even just go vote against MAGA, then this book was a success!

Feel free to reach out to me at russell@magaterrorism.com or visit www.magaterrorism.com.

"There is nothing so likely to produce peace as to be well prepared to meet an enemy."

George Washington - Mount Vernon, January 29, 1780[1]

PREFACE

FIRST OF ALL, this book is for you.

I want you to have a full understanding of how the "Make America Great Again" (MAGA) movement and its supporters may affect your life and your freedoms. How they may terrorize you to do this. How to refute their impassioned, but verifiably false, "truths." And last, but not least, how to stop them.

I wrote this book as a cautionary statement and as a call to action. The facts that support me are readily available to any open mind that seeks them out. I always encourage intelligent, factual debate and do my best to keep an open mind as well. We all have tendencies to want to believe certain things are true, only to find out later some are not. Being open-minded means sometimes you must change how you think based on factual information.

All my information is open source (publicly available). Much of it is readily accessible in the media. I have included references to support all my facts. MAGA loves to ask for your sources! This book will provide them.

In contrast, even if you find them in the nonfiction section, most MAGA books are as fictional as they come.

As for my experience with this topic, I am a retired law enforcement officer (LEO), having proudly served my country for over thirty years—twenty as a federal agent with the US Department of Homeland Security (DHS), specifically as a counterterrorist, and five prior years as a federal police officer. I joined the US Army National Guard at eighteen with a military occupational specialty of military police. I served over five years in the National Guard and was deployed overseas for Operation Desert Storm and later became an officer and led a platoon.

I have had many full- and part-time adjunct assignments as an instructor. I taught soldiers, police officers, federal agents, and other LEOs and stakeholders (civilians we directly work with) for many years. This included a considerable amount of training in, and teaching of, both foreign and domestic counterterrorism methods, tactics, and techniques. It wasn't just theoretical either. We all used these skills out in the real world.

The reason I mention my resume is that it is relevant to two critical questions: What makes me an expert on terrorism, and why should you listen to me?

We will discuss throughout the book how a deliberate misinformation campaign has been implemented to sow doubt about the veracity of any claim, no matter how wildly obvious it is, or how well it is backed by factual information. There are right-wing "news" organizations that have touted so many knowingly false comments[2] as to possibly exceed the number of times Trump did so while in office—over 30,000 false or misleading claims in four years.[3]

PREFACE

I am proud of the work I did to protect the American people. I am not selling myself to be more than I am. There are many others who have done more, and sacrificed more, than I ever have or will. We all owe them our thanks for protecting us and our country, even if they were later indoctrinated into a viewpoint that is the antithesis of their promise to the American people. Hopefully this will bring some of them back to their duty to defend the Constitution. It will also help us to understand how this indoctrination can occur in those sworn to protect our Constitution. It has twenty-seven amendments now, not just the first ten.

I wanted to explain this up front so you understand that the statements I make in this book are based on my vast, personal experience. And that my duty to my oath of office (that every member of the armed forces and federal civilian employee takes) has deeply affected me and others like me. I am not a lone voice.

Please join me.

CHAPTER ONE
INTRODUCTION

I WANTED TO START BY JUST HAVING a conversation with you. As a former instructor, it's weird to be writing instead of talking. Let me explain how this book came to be. I didn't dream of writing this book; I felt compelled to.

The last twenty years of my career, I worked as a federal air marshal. I am very proud of that. I am proud I was entrusted to protect you. What I am not proud of is the actions of some of my fellow agents. That is, in part, what led to this book. I want you to know that I, and many other agents, had to endure (or are still enduring) working with fellow agents who were (or are) openly supportive of MAGA. Needless to say, speaking up against them while I was in the government was less than effective. And painful. Especially since many of them were, or are still, in supervisory positions. I had to wait until I was retired to tell you what I learned and experienced.

Why did I wait? Because I could not tell you that I was a federal air marshal (FAM) while still working as an undercover agent, for obvious reasons. To understand how closely I worked with agents who openly identified with MAGA, I must disclose that I am a retired FAM. Will I face retaliation? Almost certainly. But our country is worth it. Protecting our constitutional rights is worth it.

I wanted you to have a firsthand account of working not just against MAGA, but of having to work with agents who are MAGA. This is personal. Not just for me, but for you also. Their actions are affecting our lives, not just theirs. It is one thing to express your opinions as a civilian, like I am now, and another altogether to do so while in uniform, on duty, or in an official capacity.

It is implied that the actions of federal law enforcement personnel represent more than just that of a single person. Our individual actions reflect the department and our government. It is important because our actions (or lack thereof) represent police and government in general and affect how the public perceives us. I think we can agree, it is safe to say the government and police are fighting an image problem already.

Here is an anecdote of something that happened that is just one example of why I had to write this book and spread its message far and wide:

While I was on duty and in uniform, I was with a team of uniformed agents performing counterterrorism duties. We had stopped to eat in a public venue. At a table near us, some women sat down. One appeared to be a transgender woman.

Several members of the team were pro-MAGA, and some of them started loudly talking about transgender people in a very negative way, specifically mentioning disgust for men trying to look like women. It should be noted that it was only some of the pro-MAGA

INTRODUCTION

members of my team that were involved in the transphobic taunts.

As you can imagine, hearing several heavily armored and armed police officers talking about them in public with many people around made them extremely upset. The distressed look on their faces, and the faces of many bystanders, was evident. One of my fellow agents, also disgusted by some of my team's behavior, joined me in loudly telling those MAGA agents that they needed to stop and that their actions were unacceptable for federal employees and police officers. They continued unabated.

The other agent and I talked with the women, apologized on behalf of the government, and told them that they were safe. We stopped eating and stood apart from our team.

Can you imagine being in their position? Here is a group of police officers, all men, mostly 200-plus pounds, armed and in full heavy gear, intimidating you. It must have been terrifying. If you were there and reading this now, I want you to know that many of us, in (or formerly in) the government, are also against MAGA. And that no apology can ever make up for their behavior that day.

Those MAGA agents negatively represented the government, the police, and me. I am glad that one of the agents joined me against them. Shout out to you, you know who you are.

I will not allow these types of pro-MAGA activities to stand. Nor should you. Police are duty bound to protect all Americans regardless of their backgrounds or beliefs. I wish a civilian had reported this event when it happened.

Well, I am a civilian now. So I don't have to hold back. I can't share classified information or agents' identities, but otherwise I can tell you about things that happened while I was working with them.

While I was working with MAGA.

CHAPTER TWO
BUT I *AM* MAGA

YOU CAN SKIP AHEAD to Chapter Three if you are not with MAGA. However, I think this chapter is still a good read for anyone (but I am biased). So, keep in mind, in this chapter only, I am speaking directly to MAGA supporters, who I refer to as MAGA.

I am going to assume, for a moment, that if you are MAGA that this may be the only chapter you are going to read before returning my book to the shelf. I hope I am wrong. Thank you for being open-minded enough to read this. I know you will not like many things in this book. But I hope you come to the realization that, like what I say or not, the information in this book is both accurate and factual. It has been exhaustively fact-checked and the sources are there for you to verify my claims.

Before we start, can we agree on something?

America and the Constitution are inseparable. You cannot be a good American and defy the Constitution at the same time. Do we agree? If so, please read on …

MAGA and I have had too many arguments with too little facts (at the ready) to back them up, for too long. That is the purpose of this book—to provide easy-to-find facts in one quickly accessible place. I have read books on many of my enemies in the past. I have read an extreme version of the Quran.[4] I have read terrorist group manifestos. Take the time to read and analyze my book.

If you still feel I am an enemy, at least you will have good "ammo" to fight me with. And a much better understanding of why others don't agree with the concept of a "patriotic" MAGA member. I look forward to any intelligent debate and constructive criticism.

Let me start by saying we are more alike than you may think. Sure, I have strong feelings against MAGA. That is clear in the title of my book. But the title is not "Republicans suck" or "We should all be Democrats."

I am a patriot, and I am sure you feel the same way. We both care deeply about America. I was a proud member of our government, and I did my part to thwart those who are enemies of our country. Those who infringe upon the freedom and liberty of our people. Those who break the law.

Many of you have done the same. Many MAGA are police and military (or former). Thank you for your service. I really mean that. American police and military members will always be my brothers-and-sisters-in-arms.

On many days, we did a lot of good things for America and its people. Let's not stop. It is not too late to take a cold, hard look at what protecting *all* the Constitution looks like. Or, at the very least, I hope to show that the goals of MAGA and a liberal democracy are mutually exclusive. The Constitution, as it exists today, does not allow for many of the things you want. It would need to be amended, by law, to repeal (in part or in whole) many of our amendments past the first ten (the Bill of Rights), and even two of the first ten. What parts?

Amendment One (freedom of speech, press, religion, peaceful assembly, and the right to petition the government for a redress of grievances), Amendment Nine (the enumeration of certain rights shall not deny or disparage other rights retained by the people), Amendment Twelve (Congress's ratification of the vote for president of the United States [POTUS] and Vice President of the United States [VPOTUS], which MAGA violated on January 6), Amendment Fourteen (the limitation on insurrectionists holding any federal or state position, a.k.a. office), Amendment Fifteen (the right of every adult male to vote, and Congress's enforcement of this right), Amendment Nineteen (women's right to vote), and Amendment Twenty (when POTUS's term ends, he can't attempt a self-coup to extend it unlawfully).

Depending on how regressive you want to be, to bring America back to its "greatness" of the past, perhaps also parts of Amendments Thirteen (abolition of slavery) and Amendment Twenty-two (the two-term POTUS limit) would need to go.

I do not say these things flippantly or to aggravate you.

You are not, legally and validly, going to get those votes to amend the Constitution. You just aren't. Not in a liberal democracy. On that note, "liberal" has nothing to do with left wing or Democrat in this context. I'm referring to liberal democracy[5], which is a multiparty system of at least two viable political parties and a system of checks and balances from several, independent branches of government. No one party has complete control.

I have worked with MAGA supporters in the government for many years. I get the desire to be patriotic and to do what you feel is right. But we have safeguards in this country when it comes to forcing others to behave like us against their will. Unless it is illegal, Americans are free to act in the way they want, even if it may go against your personal beliefs.

They can use the bathroom of their gender identity.

They can travel to a different state for any reason.

They can read all books even if you, or I, don't like the subject matter.

They can talk about, and even teach, how America has done some dark and evil things (as almost all countries have).

Importantly, they can teach facts. Even if you, or I, don't like what those facts are. And, most importantly, they are *not* to be taught flat-out lies.

The earth is not 6,000 years old. It is important to note many MAGA do not believe this either. But I have met extremist pseudo-Christian MAGA members who do believe that. There is also no undeniable, physical proof of an all-powerful being. You can still believe, but it must be taken on faith.

The Bible is a book of faith. It even says right in it that it must be taken on faith:

> Hebrews 11:1, from the King James Version (KJV) Bible, says, "Now faith is the substance of things hoped for, the evidence of things not seen."[6]

America in the eighteenth and nineteenth centuries did commit genocide on the indigenous population. According to an article on History.com, Native Americans numbered between five and fifteen million in 1492 when Columbus arrived. After the United States authorized over 1,500 attacks on Indians, their numbers were down to less than 238,000 by the end of the nineteenth century.[7]

America, after the Thirteenth Amendment was ratified into law in 1865, still mistreated and racially persecuted people of color for over a century since then. An entry in *Encyclopedia of Alabama* explains in detail the many actions that justify this conclusion. Feel free to read the article if you have any doubts about this time in American history. We will cover the treatment of Blacks in America during this time in Chapter Five also.[8]

The reason I mention these things is because I believe that MAGA has supported only teaching what it wants taught, not the "whole truth" of events that have occurred in America's past. Rewriting history doesn't change what actually happened. We will talk in depth about the Republicans' efforts to ban books in a later chapter also. The only reason to ban books is to silence the First Amendment and not let ideas you don't agree with see the light of day.

I beseech you to see the error of your ways in following and supporting MAGA. Truly, I do. If you want a right-wing agenda, please vote for it. That is what America is about. But if you are using threats, intimidation, or violence, you need to stop right now. That is very *un*-American. Hundreds of MAGA are in jail right now because of their actions. And they are there because they broke the law, and they deserve to be there. Full stop.

One of the things that we can learn from history is this:

If you support evil, then even if you win, you lose.

Had Germany and the Nazi Party been successful in WWII, the common person supporting them would not have won. Sure, the people at the very top would have had it made. But everyone else, even the most faithful SS, would not have had free speech, or even lived a life without constant fear of the government. What about any persons that are despised and unwanted, due to their identity or beliefs, in the new regime? They would have been lucky to exist at all.

Does this example of a fascist government sound good to you? A government with complete control by a single party?

If it does, then you are a terrible American. I have a copy of the US Constitution sitting beside me right now. Please get one and read it. *Really* read it.

Pursue your goals legally and do not use violence or intimidation to reach them, especially on your fellow Americans! It is a reasonable demand.

Oh, and if you are one of the MAGA that is getting ready to give a bad review or scathing comment about this book, please do! We still have the freedom to say what we want, as of now.

But I also ask that you do this:

I was taught that criticism is worthless without offering solutions. So, instead of just saying, "This is liberal, woke garbage!" (perhaps in all caps?), say *why* it is. Give factual examples of how something in this book is incorrect, and how you are right, and of how the Constitution and liberal democracy can survive intact under MAGA rule.

Right now, I just don't see how that is possible.

CHAPTER THREE
IDENTIFYING AND FIXING THE PROBLEM

BEFORE WE CAN GET INTO fighting MAGA, we first need to identify who and what we are fighting. And why. This is something I have decades of experience with. We need to study and research our enemy.

Is calling them an enemy too harsh?

Do you consider al-Qaeda to be an enemy? Al-Qaeda's stated goal is to have foreign countries, and what it considers to be corrupt Islamic regimes, out of Islamic lands. They have declared holy war against the United States.[9]

And they have attacked us on our home soil.

What about MAGA? According to *Encyclopaedia Britannica Online*, its stated goal is in its name, "Make America Great Again." Supporters want to change America into their vision of it at all costs.

They consider America, as it is now, a failure. They want to make it great again by establishing a version where extremist Republicans "encourage or enforce what MAGA members consider to be traditional American values." And they want to have complete control of federal, state, and local governments.[10]

On the topic of "traditional American values" is the rise in Christian nationalism and its support for Trump and MAGA. Paul D. Miller wrote an excellent article in *Christianity Today*, "What is Christian Nationalism?" In my opinion, we see this in their support for a leader who is not what many would consider "a good Christian," but support him anyway for advancing their cause, even though MAGA has used violence and intimidation to achieve this.[11]

And they have attacked us on our home soil.

According to a bipartisan Senate report, approximately 140 police officers were injured during the January 6, 2021, attack on our country, and seven individuals, including three law enforcement officers, ultimately died.[12]

Let that sink in.

Does MAGA sound like it meets the criteria of a domestic terrorist organization?

If so, let's look at how we fight them. Throughout this book, I am going to break down any claims, sometimes using specific facts and definitions, and sometimes just logic. Then I am going to question you to decide—is what I say proven or not?

I want to emphasize that I am using facts as the basis for this book. Our entire message against MAGA is that of truth and facts versus lies and misinformation.

Let's start by defining a few terms that are commonly used in our conversations about MAGA.

You will hear the term "woke" or "woke agenda" often in this book. *Merriam-Webster* describes woke as being "aware of and actively attentive to societal facts and issues (especially issues of racial and social justice)." It is used as an insult by MAGA supporters to describe liberal political opponents.

What is terrorism and counterterrorism? Per *Merriam-Webster*, terrorism is "the systematic use of terror, especially as a means of coercion."

Counterterrorism is defined as "measures designed to combat or prevent terrorism."[13]

What is MAGA?

MAGA is an acronym for "Make America Great Again." It is a movement based on the political slogan of its acknowledged leader, Donald Trump. According to an excellent article in *Encyclopaedia Britannica Online*, MAGA supporters believe America has lost status due to immigration from developing countries, globalization of the economy, and foreign influence. They are proponents of an "America First" doctrine that espouses economic protectionism through isolationism, reduced immigration from "undesirable" countries, and enforcing what they believe to be traditional American values. For example, in 2015 Trump called for a shutdown of Muslims entering the United States.[14]

MAGA supporters have been known to have a combative character and use belligerent language, have controversial rhetoric and beliefs, and employ the use of both legal and illegal methods to enforce those beliefs. They are extremely partisan and generally not inclusive of those who do not think like they do. Their messages and actions have been criticized as sexist, racist, anti-LGBTQ+, and for inciting violence. They view the mainstream media with contempt and feel that they are spreading lies about MAGA and working against their cause, or for their enemies. Because of this, they are susceptible to false news stories that are spread by far-right media and MAGA leaders. They generally shun news that is outside of their prescribed media sources.[15]

So let us assume for argument's sake that MAGA is a terrorist movement.

At the end of this book, I will discuss how to apply five steps specifically to fight MAGA terrorism.

Yes, both the military and civilian governments have standard operating procedures (SOPs) and their own methodologies for fighting these enemies. And yes, it is generally classified or at least sensitive information. They won't be discussed here, in specific terms, for these reasons:

I can't talk about classified/sensitive intelligence (to include specific methodology we used).

I can't talk about other methodologies used because I don't know them. Why? Because I didn't have a need to know, and it wasn't shared with me. That is how classified information is supposed to work. More on someone charged with the illegal mishandling and misusing of classified information in a later chapter.

CHAPTER FOUR
PSEUDO-PATRIOTISM

I WANT US TO CONTINUE HAVING a mutual understanding of the words we will use throughout this book—not to be pedantic, but just to make sure we're on the same page regarding their meanings.

First up is the word "pseudo," a combining form meaning false or pretended; not actually but having the appearance of or trying to be. A sham, in other words.

This is usually combined with another word to infer that it is an untrue version of that base word. It is mimicking or trying to pretend to be something that it is not. In effect, adopting the original meaning with one that is false.

"Patriotism" is another term for national loyalty. The devotion of support, love, and defense of that country.[16]

"Pseudo-patriotism," according to Dictionary.com, is not a word.

Maybe it should be?

For the purposes of this book, we will also use "pseudo" to describe religious people who share a false, sham version of what billions of people believe in. A version supporting terrorism for the sake of *their* version of Christianity or Islam, or whatever other belief system they may follow. You will see them described here as "pseudo-Christians" and "pseudo-Muslims." Why? Because it understandably bothers true Christians and Muslims to be associated with this vicious scum.

In my last few years as an agent, I realized just how bad a MAGA problem the US government really has. Imagine working to protect the rights of *all* people in America, for decades, only to see some of your own fellow government colleagues mistreating those Americans. Then watching counterterrorists openly support a movement that uses the methods of terrorism against our own country. And seeing some of your fellow citizens feverishly working to undo the parts of the Constitution they don't like and break down the checks and balances of our government to destroy liberal democracy in America. This has taken a toll on me. This book is my, and yours if you wish, response to the endless excuses for the behavior and false reasonings of the MAGA movement.

My biggest fear is that MAGA's attack on America is not being taken seriously enough. We can no longer fly our American flag or wear it across our chests without fearing we will be perceived as Trump and MAGA supporters.

I believe they have co-opted our symbols of patriotism. But I need to show you the sources that support that belief, so let's read on …

OK, what is the definition of "co-opted"? According to Dictionary.com, it is the taking over, or appropriating, as one's own.[17]

PSEUDO-PATRIOTISM

Is that not what you think when you see a person with a flag now? Have our symbols of patriotism been co-opted from us? When you see someone with the American flag, is your first thought, "They are probably pro-Trump, or pro-MAGA"? A lot of the time they will include other symbolism to show their loyalty as well. How many times do you see an American flag with a "TRUMP for President" or "MAGA" statement along with it? Often MAGA will fly their flag at the same height as our nation's flag, in violation of the guideline that the American flag should always fly above others.[18] And the idea of a secessionist flag like that of the Confederacy being flown along with, or even in the presence of, the American flag? There is no symbolism more anti-American than that flag.

I believe they have taken a patriotic symbol, the flag of the United States of America, and co-opted it to the point where it is often viewed as synonymous with MAGA or "pseudo-patriotism." According to an article in NBC News, there was another group who co-opted our nation's flag for their own political purposes: the Nazis. The German American Bund (a pro-Nazi group) held a rally at Madison Square Garden in 1939. Over 20,000 people attended and raised their right arms in a Nazi salute as an oversized American flag passed by them in the procession. Ancient history some people might say. But usurping our nation's flag for an unpatriotic purpose is clearly not unprecedented. In my opinion, MAGA attaching themselves onto our flag, like a parasite, is just as disgusting now as it was then with the Nazis.[19]

How often, in contrast, do you see a flag with a quote about defending democracy from MAGA, or from the Republicans who support them? How about seeing "Biden for President" along with that flag? Why not?

Because we know MAGA supporters are willing to deface our property, or verbally or physically attack us.

We fear retaliation for exercising our First Amendment right to free speech. To put up signs, or bumper stickers, or even just talk publicly about it. Why?

One word—terrorism.

While I was training my fellow agents after the 2020 election was over and Joe Biden had been sworn in, I witnessed many inappropriate actions by federal employees. These were agents who were on duty, I would like to add.

For example, I saw them wearing and displaying the far-right symbology of the MAGA movement. I saw Punisher skulls and "Q" on MAGA supporters' clothing and bags, while on duty.

An article by the American University in Washington, DC, explained how the MAGA movement uses symbology to show their allegiance to the movement:

These Punisher skulls are purported to have started as a symbol of support for righting wrongs that traditional law enforcement could not. The symbol has also been adopted by some members of the military. But now it has been adopted by groups on the far right, such as the Proud Boys and Oath Keepers, to symbolize the failure of law enforcement to address the concerns of the people. Maybe this explains why MAGA, with its supposed support of law and order, attacked the police? What it doesn't explain is why some police were, or are, wearing them. Or maybe it does?

The "Q" insignia stands for QAnon affiliation. QAnon started in 2016 with an alleged mysterious government insider who had a fringe conspiracy theory that a secret alliance of Democrats and prominent media figures, who are pedophiles, are conspiring to take over the world. Early adopters were primarily Trump supporters but now also include some anti-lockdown Libertarians and evangelical psuedo-Christians.[20] Sounds pretty insane, right? I talked with one, a fellow agent no less, and they actually believe this stuff.

I also saw "We the People Are Pissed Off" on a cap (referring to election denial), and I listened to relentless bashing of anything that wasn't in line with MAGA thinking.

"Let's Go Brandon!" (otherwise known as "F**k Joe Biden") was spoken aloud by agents while at work at my field office, even after President Biden was sworn in.

"Let's Go Brandon" came into being when a reporter at Talladega Superspeedway in Alabama misheard people chanting "F**k Joe Biden" and thought they were saying "Let's Go Brandon." Brandon Brown was the Sparks 300 race winner that day. It spread quickly among the MAGA culture and become a common phrase within the Republican Party and MAGA. It was even said on the US House floor by a Republican.[21]

Do you think what happened at that stadium was massive political intimidation?

Do you think it was meant to cow Democrats into silence?

What if we went to a NASCAR event, started a chant of "F**k you, MAGA," and then waited to see what would happen next. Do you think the pro-MAGA people there would applaud our First Amendment rights even though they disagree with us? Or do you think it would turn violent?

One of my MAGA-supporter colleagues liked to say he was "taking a Pelosi" when he went to the bathroom. Hahaha, what's the harm in that? This is: In San Francisco, a federal jury convicted a man of breaking into the Pelosi home and attacking Paul Pelosi, husband of former House Speaker Nancy Pelosi, with a hammer. He was attempting to assault Nancy Pelosi, but her husband was home instead. He fractured Paul's skull with that hammer.

This MAGA terrorist thought of himself as a patriot. Now he is going to go to prison.[22]

Angry rhetoric against left-leaning politicians and LGBTQ+ people was a common refrain from MAGA supporters I worked with daily. And yes, even racism reared its ugly head. One MAGA supporter compared the riot in Portland to the insurrection at the Capitol. The Portland riot was over the killing of a Black man, George Floyd, at the hands of law enforcement.[23] The irony here is that this riot in Portland was a centerpiece of Trump's "law and order" reelection campaign. And the Capitol riot, which was also a lawless riot, happened under his watch. And not only did it happen under his watch, but he even encouraged it to happen, as we will cover later in this book. So, the MAGA supporter said to me that the woman (Ashli Babbitt) who was shot by US law enforcement at the Capitol was murdered.[24] But he was completely OK with excessive force being used by police in Portland.

Many of my MAGA colleagues were vociferous supporters of putting down the riot in Portland but supported the insurrection at the Capitol. They simultaneously claimed they were pro-police, even though police were injured and killed on January 6. They also voiced their support of an alleged career criminal whose aspirations to become an autocrat are well known. Trump has openly praised the rule of Kim Jong Un and Vladimir Putin.[25]

I am not perfect, nor do I pretend to be. I have had bad thoughts at times, we all have. But I realize that is what they are, and I strive to do the right thing despite them. Whenever I was on duty, in uniform or undercover, I always remembered I was there to protect *all* people. Even the ones I had to arrest. I didn't give in to "street justice." I did my best to use as little force as necessary. What about the ones I didn't like? Irrelevant. I deliberately thought to myself, "Pretend you are always being watched or filmed, are you doing the right thing? Not only legally, but morally and reflecting of my profession with honor." Did I always succeed perfectly? No. But I did my best.

I respect the rights of others, even if they disagree with me. I accept the results of free and fair elections, even if I don't like them. That is patriotism.

Calling the election, and thus the government, fake and illegitimate; attacking the Capitol while Congress is ratifying the vote (per the Twelfth Amendment of the Constitution); supporting insurrection and intimidating and threatening people who disagree with you—even going so far as to construct gallows outside the Capitol for the vice president, surrounded by rioters chanting "Hang Mike Pence."[26]

This is the opposite of patriotism. It is tyranny.

Sadly, the number of converts I have talked away from the MAGA movement as of now is still zero.

That is how deeply entrenched they are in this movement. How indoctrinated and brainwashed they are.

That is dangerous for us all.

CHAPTER FIVE
AMERICA, LAND OF THE FREE

WHAT MAKES AMERICA the Land of the Free? Two things are critical for sure—the Constitution of the United States and the existence of our liberal democracy.

America. I cannot tell you how much pride I have in this word. I am proud of the American flag, the one with fifty stars not thirteen (the flag of the Confederacy). I am proud to tell others I am an American. I am proud to be an American, but a modern one. Not the one from 200 years ago.

I still cherish our liberal democracy and our freedoms under the Constitution. I am no longer employed as a counterterrorist, but we can all use words to fight terrorism.

And we will.

MAGA are saying America isn't great and that their way of changing it will fix that. They are also, very loudly, saying that anyone who is not MAGA is unpatriotic and a bad American, and only "true" MAGA supporters can be patriots. How do I know this? Because I have witnessed it firsthand. For many years. I imagine you have as well.

But what is their patriotic, American way?

In my opinion, it is making sure we lose our liberal democracy and change it into a failed democracy system. Whereby reactionary right-wing ideals are made into laws of the land, with an autocratic dictator at the top. Many MAGA I have talked to have an idealized dream of an America as it was. They claim the failure of America is because we are at the mercy of "liberal ideals." They want the "American Dream" back!

What can they do to stop these liberal ideals? Well, first is to obtain effective control by one party—the Republicans—and then to fight against the "woke agenda."

When it comes to the "American Dream," there are some things to remember about what made it possible for so many in America's past. Let's look at what can be derived from an article in *The Atlantic*. The article shows that the "success" of our country "back then" was on the backs of those America had largely oppressed for many generations: indigenous peoples, immigrants, people of color, and women. What made us "great" back then is that it was great to be a successful, usually White, man with a "nuclear" family. The idealized version of this refers to a household consisting of a father who works and can afford to have a mother stay at home to take care of household affairs and the children.

I want to add that many of these people, both White and non-White, had to work hard to succeed and that many of them in that generation did not harbor any ill will toward others. However, there is no denying the systemic "leg up" because of the events of previous generations. Part of this was also America's advantageous financial position after WWII relative to other countries. The combination of these two factors is what made this "American Dream" possible for the average income earner. These disparities have decreased, especially over the last several decades. This is a good thing when it comes to discrimination. Wealth becoming more equally shared, combined with America not having as much of an advantage in the world economy, has led to the loss of the financial situation that allows for this "one-income family" for most Americans.[27]

So, how do I know of such a "great" America? Because it is what I had as a child. My dad worked and my mom stayed home to raise my brother and me. A one-income household in an upper-middle-class neighborhood.

Then, by the 1980s, this "ideal" household began to fray. Inflation had pushed up the costs of living to the point that my mother had to go back to work also.

This "American Dream" that is idealized by MAGA? At this point, it requires well over $100,000 a year in income, and just the man earning it. Plus, a woman, young and fertile enough to have children, living at home. And home means detached home, with a yard, in a nice and safe neighborhood. The kind I grew up in where I could go visit my friends and our mothers would meet up and have coffee and relax.

Sound familiar today? Didn't think so.

MAGA wants their version of the "American Dream" back.

Am I making this up about MAGA to make them look bad?

Turns out, no. They even have a new term for a stay-at-home mom who acts (and some even dress) like it's the 1950s: trad wife.

A trad wife is used to describe a woman that believes in and practices a traditional sexual role and *submissive* position in a traditional marriage. It is the combining of the word traditional with wife or housewife.[28]

Doesn't sound like a bad or evil thing to be, right?

What is unsaid, in my opinion, is that world only existed, in part, because of the oppressed being underpaid and undervalued so that the "American Dream" winners could live in luxury, while the oppressed suffered to create it. Do you think the average American man has the economic means to support this lifestyle today? Nope. It is as much a status symbol now as living in a fancy house (or any house at this point) or driving a fancy car.

In my opinion, it also says something else. It says that if you don't support traditional sex roles and marriage, you are not a good person. How can I say this? Because some trad wives, and their husbands, support MAGA in its goal to punish those who do not live their pseudo-Christian version of Christianity. Not only that, but I don't think they are inclusive of other religions in this trad wife movement, as it is mostly conservative Christians who belong to it.

I am *not* saying that being a stay-at-home parent (man or woman) is a bad thing. It is the implied demand of submissiveness of women toward men, and the bigotry toward others who do not share their views, that I have a problem with.

Maybe take a look at their MAGA views on LGBTQ+ and nontraditional relationships. It is not evil to want to live as a trad wife if your family can afford it and both the husband and wife believe in and support its values. What is evil are all the laws being passed against the people who do not share their views. According to the Human Rights Campaign, there have been a record number of anti-LGBTQ+ bills introduced in state legislatures. Over 520 in the first five months of 2023 alone. These are bills that can become laws, which are oppressing these groups all over again, just as America was finally starting to be seen as a beacon of hope for the oppressed and downtrodden …[29]

Am I "woke"? Is this the kind of liberal dogma that MAGA is talking about? Yes. Guilty as charged.

I will never fall into a specific political ideal. Do I feel I, personally, owe someone else because of the sins of my forefathers? No, I don't. And MAGA feels the same way.

The difference between them and me (and hopefully you also!) is that we realize the harms that were done to make this "American Dream" possible. And there is a moral imperative to, at least, fix obvious wrongs. MAGA is busy making its Republican leaders pass laws to ban books and keep our kids "safe" from learning "inconvenient truths" so as not to upset them, or to make them believe these things never happened and America has never committed any wrongs in the past. What proof is there of this? According to an article in American Progress Action, Republican-led states banned more than 1,000 books in schools. Several studies show a link between stronger gun laws keeping kids safer, but none show that banning books does.[30]

Banning books. And here we thought Ray Bradbury's *Fahrenheit 451*[31] was fiction, not a prognostication of America's possible future.

The United States has a long history of denying loans (both small business and home ownership) and employment (or underpaying for a similar job when they got one) to minorities and immigrants. And of putting new highways and roads, using imminent domain, through communities of color, destroying neighborhoods and homes.[32]

I am not saying I owe cash directly from my paycheck to pay someone's great, great grandson because my great, great grandfather killed Native Americans. Instead of giving MAGA what it wants, which is cutting programs to help the middle and lower class while helping the upper class, why not instead invest tax dollars to help the majority of Americans who are not wealthy?[33] The money should go toward the programs they are trying to cut, instead of away from them. Things like making sure that kids can eat healthy food at lunch or have laptops during the next pandemic. Or helping with everything from education and health care to public safety. Help "fix" neighborhoods that we put that road through. That is not just being woke. That is having empathy and doing what is right. In other words, being a good person.

Entire nonfiction books have been written about the mistreatment of Black people, women, immigrants, and other minorities in America. So, we will only touch on it long enough to give MAGA another example of facts not being on their side.

The "American Dream" we discussed? Here is a timeline of just a small piece of America's shameful past. It's about the "American Dream" most Black people "enjoyed" in our country:

In 1793 the Fugitive Slave Act was passed. This act made it a federal crime to assist the escape of an enslaved person.

In 1863, in an effort to preserve the Union, President Lincoln freed the slaves in the south. Think about that. His Emancipation Proclamation only freed the enslaved people in the rebel states, not in the north or the border states.[34] In fact, in his last speech on April 11, 1865, he expressed his preference that some "colored men"—the "very intelligent, and on those who serve our cause as soldiers"— have the right to vote.[35]

In 1865, the Thirteenth Amendment was passed, officially abolishing slavery.

From 1865 to 1877 was the time period known as Reconstruction. During this period, Black Americans started to gain influence. They had started to win elections into southern governments and the US Congress. This caused distress to many White southerners. They felt they were losing control and began creating protective societies such as the Ku Klux Klan (KKK). The use of terrorism against Black people became more widespread.[36]

In 1868, the Fourteenth Amendment broadened the definition of citizenship, granting "equal protection" of the Constitution to people who had been enslaved.

In 1870, the Fifteenth Amendment made it illegal to deny one's ability to vote based on their previous condition of servitude or race.

By 1885, most schools in the southern states were separated into Black and White.[37]

In 1896, in the landmark case of *Plessy v. Ferguson*, the US Supreme Court upheld a Louisiana law that required segregation of passengers on railway cars. They ruled that as long as the conditions were separate but equal, persons could be separated based on race—the "separate but equal" doctrine.[38]

By 1900 many establishments, such as restaurants, theaters, barber shops, and public transportation, required White people to be separated from any person of color. Kind of like when your friend sits in first class, and you are in coach. Separate but equal.

In 1954 came the *Brown v. Board of Education* decision. We are, finally, getting somewhere. The US Supreme Court ruled that racial segregation in public schools was a violation of the Fourteenth Amendment.[39]

In 1955, Rosa Parks, a Black woman, refused to give up her seat to a White man when asked to by the city bus driver. Good for her! But this was a crime and, of course, she was arrested for violating the law that Black passengers sit in the back of public buses and give up their seats to White people if the front seats are full.[40]

This is just a small period of time and isn't even an exhaustive list of all that occurred. Do you think these events actually happened? Or are they "fake news"? Intelligent, reasonable people know these events actually happened, but how we react to these events is biased by our personal worldview and our belief systems.

As you can see, the plight of Black people in America wasn't "solved" by the Emancipation Proclamation of 1863. People who weren't even counted as "people" until 1865 and couldn't vote until 1870.

How many of these laws were passed by America's first version of MAGA (MAG?) to continue oppressing a minority group? Guess who openly supports MAGA?

According to an article in *The Nation*, The KKK and White supremacy groups.[41]

For almost 100 years into the history of our "great" country, Black people were slaves. For almost a hundred years after that, from when they were "freed," unconstitutional laws continued to be passed, many by a group of mostly southern, former Confederate, states. The same ones who today support MAGA to bring back the "great" America of the 1950s and earlier.[42]

Oh, and women? In 1920, the Nineteenth Amendment was ratified into the Constitution, which allowed women to vote. So, they didn't really start their journey as equals until over 140 years after the founding of our country. That is the "great" country in "Make America Great Again."

So, going back to trad wives. Based on the information we have discussed, I think many of these trad wives believe that they do not sacrifice women's rights by choosing a subservient role in their marriage, but in my opinion, they do. As I mentioned before, you can be a "homemaker" and a stay-at-home partner (man or woman) and not have to defer to the "man of the house" as a second-class citizen.

Let's start by defining a simple word, "objectify." Quite simply it means to degrade someone to the status of a mere object. In this case, a very sexist viewpoint.

What they are doing is encouraging the objectification of women. There is nothing inherently wrong about being a trad wife, except that it is voluntarily accepting second-class status to men. After over 100 years of working to be equals. Staying home to take care of the home and children? Totally OK. Having to defer to the man because you are a woman? Not OK at all.

Do you see a similarity between the mistreatment of minorities for financial gain then and now? Do you think MAGA's continued assault on nonbelievers (those that don't share their extreme version of pseudo-Christianity) isn't eerily similar to the KKK doctrine that supports White power? Except it is now applied to anyone who is against MAGA, not just Black people.

It is sad that we must work so hard to do what is right and stop evil in our own country, even today. Thank you MAGA, for trying to force us back to the "good old days."

Despicable.

CHAPTER SIX
OK, NOW WHAT?

NOW WE KNOW WHO THEY ARE, what they want, and how they operate. At least a little. We will learn more as we go. But how do we stop them? Knowledge is power. If it is used.

The first thing to do is to make as many people as possible aware of the severity of the threat. I believe that MAGA is a greater threat to our liberal democracy than any other organization in the world.

No other organization has done as much to infiltrate and control our federal, state, and local governments as MAGA has. Its members are in our executive, legislative, and judicial branches. They are in both our civilian and military governments. And they are growing in power. They are passing laws in line with their agenda, and blocking, or voting out, laws that they disagree with. An article in *The Hill* stated that Donald Trump is supported by 60–70 percent of Republican voters. Many Republicans are in government service, both military and civilian.[43]

President of the United States Joe Biden gave a speech in September 2023 about the threat of MAGA to our democracy:

> "There is something dangerous happening in America now. There is an extremist movement that does not share the basic beliefs in our democracy: the MAGA Movement … There is no question that today's Republican Party is driven and intimidated by MAGA Republican extremists."

The speech was powerful in its accuracy. POTUS said that the extremist movement known as MAGA did not share our basic democratic values and beliefs. He also said that not all Republicans are MAGA, but their party was intimidated and driven by MAGA.[44]

Now let's take a hard, unflinching look at our members of the federal government …

CHAPTER SEVEN
OATH OF OFFICE

AS A NEW SOLDIER, and again each time I took a new position as a federal employee, I swore to an oath of office on the first day of my employment. All members of Congress, the president and their cabinet, executive and judicial officers, US military members, and federal civilian employees must take similar versions of this oath to accept their position of trust to the American people.[45] This oath never ends; it does not have an expiration date, nor does it stop when you leave employment.

Below is the oath that I took. Versions for other areas of government, including POTUS and Congress, are slightly different, but all contain the same promises of preserving, protecting, and defending the Constitution of the United States.

"I will support and defend the Constitution of the United States against all enemies, foreign and domestic; that I will bear true faith and allegiance to the same; that I take this obligation freely, without any mental reservation or purpose of evasion; and that I will well and faithfully discharge the duties of the office on which I am about to enter. So help me God."[46]

Article 6 of the Constitution also says this:

"… all executive and judicial Officers, both of the United States and of the several States, shall be bound by Oath or Affirmation, to support this Constitution; but no religious Test shall ever be required as a Qualification to any Office or public Trust under the United States."[47]

So, this is saying that all positions (offices) in the executive and legislative branches shall be bound by the oath of office. This will come up later, especially in Chapter Seventeen.

The Fourteenth Amendment of the US Constitution, the Constitution those persons are now sworn to protect, says this in Section 3:

"No person shall be a Senator or Representative in Congress, or elector of President and Vice President, or hold any office, civil or military, under the United States, or under any State, who, having previously taken an oath, as a member of Congress, or as an officer of the United States, or as a member of any State legislature, or as an executive or judicial officer of any state, to support the Constitution of the United States, shall have engaged in insurrection or rebellion against the same, or given aid or comfort to the enemies thereof. But Congress may by a vote of two-thirds of each House, remove such disability."[48]

Why does this matter to us?

Well, I know firsthand that many of the federal employees I trained and worked with are openly supportive of MAGA and of the insurrection of the Capitol on January 6. Many of them believe that our election was stolen, and that Donald Trump is the "true" president. We have all, regardless of political viewpoint, seen that large parts of the Republican Party have worked with MAGA to weaken the checks and balances of our liberal democracy to consolidate their power in the government. They have infiltrated all three branches: legislative, executive, and judicial. The direction and intent are clear: to remove any part of our democracy that stands in the way of their complete control.

According to an excellent article in *Convergence*, "MAGA Authoritarian Rule or Third Reconstruction?" MAGA is pushing ahead to try and rule all three branches of government, with a dictator at the top, a.k.a. fascism. Part of what makes this so disconcerting is that they are a minority of Americans but have an outsized chance of succeeding due to voter suppression, the flawed Electoral College system, and gerrymandering. All can be used effectively to give a minority of people control of our country over a majority that does not want that. And once fascism takes control, history shows how difficult it will be to get democracy back. If we do at all.[49]

The commitment to faithfully execute the duties of your office is something every person in the US government is supposed to uphold. Does executing his duty of office seem to be something Trump places as a high priority? Or has he learned that he can abuse the office of the presidency for his personal gain and power? Has he learned how he can manipulate the court system to delay, appeal, and stonewall any violation for years? The normal checks and balances have already been weakened by Trump, and MAGA Republicans, and he has a history of intimidating or punishing anyone who stands in his way. There was a clear effort by his administration to consolidate power in the office of the presidency.[50]

Trying to separate the Grand Old Party (GOP), a.k.a. the Republican Party, the former president, and MAGA is a fool's errand. They all share the same end goal: to put Trump back in power and never have to give that power up. Even if most Americans vote against that.

Don't believe that? Review the scary last sentence of Section 3 of the Fourteenth Amendment: "But Congress may by a vote of two-thirds of each House, remove such disability."

Can you imagine an America where MAGA controls Congress and the presidency? Republicans currently have a majority in the House, and the Democrats barely lead in the Senate. There is already a conservative majority in the Supreme Court. If the Republicans, with Trump as POTUS, win in 2024, MAGA will control both the executive and legislative branches. That would be all branches of government either under MAGA's control or sympathetic to their cause.

So, am I being ridiculous? What is the big deal about Section 3? Here are some examples to consider:

Jacob Chansley, a.k.a. the QAnon Shaman, is preparing to run in the race for Congressional District 8 in Arizona. He is an ex-con who went to federal prison for his role in the January 6 Insurrection.[51]

That's correct. Now he is running as a Libertarian. A Libertarian is a person who advocates for individual liberty.[52] So, he is running on a platform that espouses civil liberty while being an ex-con that went to prison for trying to stop our votes from counting. Wish I could vote in Arizona, he is a gem! A man that may not even be able to vote in his own election is trying to become a congressman. He is still an insurrectionist by any rational interpretation. Our forefathers are rolling in their graves.

Speaking of …

A Michigan Court of Claims judge ruled that Trump can stay on the Michigan ballot, rejecting the insurrection clause challenge.[53]

The Michigan judge denied arguments that claimed Trump's role in the January 6 riot on the US Capitol meant he was ineligible for the presidency. The judge ruled that since he followed state law by qualifying for the primary ballot, he can't be removed.

Minnesota's Supreme Court also dismissed a similar challenge on technical grounds on the basis that no state statute prohibits a political party from placing a nomination on the ballot.[54]

One of the things that is so frustrating is this obvious runaround of what was intended in the Constitution. The reason that there is no mention of being allowed to run on a state ballot as an insurrectionist is because you are not supposed to be able to "hold any office, civil or military, under the United States, or under any State …"

"Or under any State." It is blatantly clear what this means. It means *no*. No, they can't be in office. In any of the fifty states in the country. Also, remember that "office" is synonymous with position or employment. So why are they allowed to run?

There is absolutely a precedent for ruling that someone is invalidated from running for office, at the state level, by federal law. You can say there is already evidence of ineligibility at the federal level and that is why the state is issuing, or concurring, the same ruling. This is why the overturning of *Roe v. Wade* was such a big deal. Justice Samuel Alito wrote on the decision (in which he voted to overturn *Roe v. Wade*, a 1973 decision):

"The inescapable conclusion is that a right to abortion is not deeply rooted in the Nation's history and traditions."[55]

OK, so that is the reason. Do you know what else is "not deeply rooted in the Nation's history and traditions"? Or, in other words, is open to being changed back to "earlier times"?

The abolition of slavery. Women's suffrage (a.k.a. right to vote). And the insurrection clause.

In that case, let's write about what he infers is OK for the Supreme Court of the United States (SCOTUS) to overturn. This is my quote of what we heard in that statement:

"The inescapable conclusion is that *any* constitutional right past the Bill of Rights is not deeply rooted in the Nation's history and traditions."

So, in other words, anything passed into law after December 15, 1791, is open to being overturned, at any time. *That* is what they are saying.

And SCOTUS has a 6–3 conservative supermajority.

So, for as long as the Fourteenth Amendment hasn't been overturned by SCOTUS, a convicted insurrectionist can't be a congressman, and a man who convinced others to riot and cause an insurrection can't be POTUS. *Not legally.*

Any judge should rule they cannot run. Stop with the semantic excuse-making. The Constitution's intent in this Amendment and Section is clear: If they "engaged in insurrection or rebellion … or given aid and comfort to …" they are ineligible to run. It doesn't say, "Only if duly convicted in a court of law," nor are they going to get convicted of "giving aid and comfort."

Even without being convicted, or even charged, I would have lost my job for the very same actions that Chansley and Trump have committed. Imagine if I got up on that podium on January 6, in police uniform, and said the things Trump did? Or, even better, imagine me fighting (assaulting) my way through other police officers, while in uniform, to invade the Capitol and stop Congress from peacefully proceeding under the direction of the Twelfth Amendment. And then wondering why I lost my job, was unable to hold a position with the federal government ever again, and was in prison.

Trump was the president of the United States at the time. He represented the entire US government. Did anyone think he was *not* acting in an official capacity? Did he announce himself as president of the United States? I think that counts, yes?

So why are we allowing Chansley and Trump to run when they couldn't hold any federal position after their actions?

Well, any federal job except for president or congressperson apparently.

Judges from two different states left it up to Congress. Are they just taking the easy way out? Maybe they are right. On principle they are only there to interpret the law. Such as the Fourteenth Amendment perhaps? Does not the state also have a right to enforce the Constitution, even if the National GOP is turning a blind eye?

SCOTUS overturned *Roe v. Wade* and states made their own constitutional protections. Why is this different? If you want to enshrine this protection, then pass it at the state level too. If Supreme Court judges can overturn laws that have been on the books for almost fifty years, I think state court judges have the authority to rule on whether the Fourteenth Amendment applies to state law.

Based on precedent, I think the scary part is that judges are potentially saying, "Don't worry about it, the GOP in Congress will ensure the Fourteenth Amendment is being followed. Just like they impartially reviewed the evidence in the two impeachments and came to the correct decision based on all the facts."

No, Chansley and Trump are not eligible for office under the Fourteenth Amendment. But, as we discussed in this book, MAGA is just going to work around the law, by having GOP in Congress vote that no law was broken at all (or more aptly, make sure no law, or motion, can pass saying the law was broken).

Maybe they will even vote, with a two-thirds majority, to just " … remove such disability."

Or SCOTUS could rule the Fourteenth Amendment doesn't apply, or better yet just overturn it.

If Trump or Chansley are allowed on the ballot, that allows them to be voted into office. That is what being on the ballot means. So, let's take a moment to think rationally.

Or not. Let's say hello to the judge in the Colorado court. District Judge Sarah B. Wallace made a decision on the applicability of the insurrection clause to the presidency.

According to *The Washington Times*, she wrote that the provision in the Fourteenth Amendment disqualifying persons engaged in insurrection (Section 3) did not apply to a president due to what she described as "scant direct evidence regarding whether the Presidency is one of the positions subject to disqualification." She also found that Trump did indeed engage in insurrection with the speech that he gave to the mob that stormed the US Capitol on January 6, 2021. She said his January 6 speech "incited imminent lawless violence," and therefore was not protected by the First Amendment.[56]

What?! So, he did engage in an insurrection according to the judge in Colorado.

"No person shall be ... or hold *any* office, civil or military under the United States, or under any state ... shall have engaged in insurrection or rebellion ..."

This is from our Constitution. There is no "other" version to look at. There is only one.

Not only does it apply to the office of the president, but it specifically states that an insurrectionist cannot hold *any* office in the US government. Any office means any job or employment.

Yes, it *does* apply to POTUS.

This makes my point. Colorado basically just said, in court:

Trump is an insurrectionist, but the Fourteenth Amendment doesn't apply to him. Even though the Constitution applies to everyone in the United States and the Amendment specifically mentions he can't hold any office under the United States. But it doesn't apply to him because the office of the presidency is exempt.

That makes sense now.

I mean, at least she ruled a state court *can* make a decision about the Fourteenth Amendment, even if it is completely wrong. How do I know it is wrong? Because the judge in Colorado ruled that Trump is an insurrectionist, and the Constitution is very specific in saying you can't hold any federal or state office as an insurrectionist. Also, after I wrote this, the Colorado Supreme Court ruled that Trump *cannot* have his name on the ballot as an insurrectionist.[57]

As of now, when I am updating this book right before it goes to publishing, SCOTUS is in talks about whether Trump should be allowed on the ballot due to states challenging that he is forbidden from doing so in the Constitution.[58] The SCOTUS justices are doing the usual back and forth instead of just saying, "Yes, he did it. Yes, he is ineligible."

Let's see what happens with this appeal to SCOTUS between the time I wrote this and now, when you are reading this book …

If Trump is voted back into office, with states like Minnesota and Michigan giving legitimacy to his eligibility to hold office, do you think our MAGA-controlled members of Congress are even going to enforce the Fourteenth Amendment? No. They will rightly say, "You allowed us to vote on them, even after the Fourteenth Amendment was brought up, so they must not have violated it." And, if you don't allow them to take office? Then MAGA will say you are trying to cancel them, and their votes don't matter. Funny how they only care about their votes, not yours.

At this point, MAGA may say something like, "But what about you, you are no different than we are?"

I have heard versions of this so many times. Just like "Hillary is a criminal too, why aren't you trying to lock her up?" Again, if she did, try her in court and, if convicted, put her in jail. Why haven't they, after all this time? Because they don't have any proof that she committed a crime. Thankfully, the courts don't put up with spin on this. You need proof guys. Hillary Clinton hasn't been successfully charged with a crime. Not once, much less 91 times … What about me trying to invalidate Republican votes? Not a chance. I would go out of my way to make sure their votes are counted, as I would do for any American.

Why would I do that?!

Because, unlike MAGA, I don't want to win at all costs. I want our liberal democracy to remain intact, of course. But I also want to enforce the Constitution *as currently written*. Not as it was when slavey was OK, and women couldn't vote. That is the "fundamental," or "originalist," view of the Constitution you hear about in Supreme Court rulings. Rulings from a conservative majority. The Bill of Rights' supporters who seem to think only the first ten amendments matter. MAGA supporters for short.

If MAGA gets control, they can legally change *every* law. And at that point, do it without any direct input from a single voter. Sure, Congress is voted in by districts of voters. However, once they are in office, we only hope they do what we ask. They don't have to. But don't worry, the 6–3 conservative supermajority (appointed by Republican presidents) in the Supreme Court will be there to rule on whether those new laws are constitutional.

Gilead, here we come ... (Gilead is a fictional theonomic, totalitarian version of a dystopian United States in the novel, *The Handmaid's Tale*, by Margaret Atwood).[59]

Now you understand why MAGA having control is the end of our liberal democracy.

So what? If I support MAGA, that is a good thing, right?

Nope.

Do MAGA supporters really think a group of rich and powerful politicians and their powerful benefactors truly care about what they want, as regular Americans, once they can control the country uncontested?

Even if MAGA wins, do you think the average person will have any options about "toeing the line" when things get really dark? When MAGA (the individuals who wanted them to have complete control) are finding out, the hard way, that they are taking away our rights for the "good of the country," will anyone be able to do anything about it?

IS MAGA A TERRORIST MOVEMENT?

I believe that MAGA is the current domestic terrorist organization that is the biggest threat to our freedoms and way of life, but the real problem is its goal and the methods being used to achieve it. I wouldn't want the Democrats creating a dictatorship or destroying liberal democracy either.

Even if you side with some of the issues MAGA supports, can you see their end goal and methods are anti-American and anti-democratic? We want our votes to count, even if it means we sometimes lose. That is democracy.

MAGA supporters have ridiculed and slandered, and some have even assaulted or threatened, anyone who does not agree or conform to their thinking. They have marginalized anyone who dares to speak against them. They have acted against groups of people they don't like and have even passed laws to punish them; we have already learned of the many bills Republican controlled states have put forth, some of which are now laws.

According to a *Politico* article, "The Threat of Civil Breakdown is Real," the US government is still underequipped to handle the MAGA threat. Mostly because of efforts by Republican political leaders to hamstring their ability to go after these domestic terrorists. And the Republicans' defense of Trump and lack of will to go after MAGA for their illegal actions, or even label them as domestic terrorists. Add to this the large number of MAGA supporters who work in the government, and we can see how this group could succeed in taking control, even as a minority of the American populace.[60]

I dedicated over thirty years of my life to protecting the US Constitution and those constitutional rights for *all* people in America. For me, this is not about right- or left-wing politics, but about the survival of our democracy.

I am sure many MAGA members will immediately decry this as "liberal" or "woke." Labeling is something that is done to discredit actual true events or facts. And people.

What bothers me so much is that, after years of protecting America and the Constitution, we are closer than we have ever been to losing the war. A war that many do not even realize is happening. We are not losing America to a foreign government, or foreign terrorist group, but to our own people who are supporting a domestic group that uses intimidation and violence. One that America hasn't yet even labeled a terrorist group. Especially worrisome is the support of MAGA by the people who are sworn to protect us from them!

People who have sworn that oath and are openly violating it. Many of whom are still employed by the federal government today.

They are, quite literally, the enemy.

CHAPTER EIGHT
TERRORISM VS. TRIBALISM

I PROMISED TO DELVE INTO HOW those in our government and military, sworn to protect the Constitution, can be indoctrinated into a group whose goals are so clearly unconstitutional. The answer is tribalism. Before we go over that though, we also need to talk about terrorism. What is it and why does MAGA use it?

We defined terrorism already by its definition as a method of warfare, but here is another definition of terrorism as it pertains to the actions of committing terrorism. It is the act of using unlawful intimidation and violence, especially against civilians, to affect political change or achieve political goals.[61]

Does this apply to the MAGA movement that was created by, and fully supports, former president Donald Trump? Do the people who support it, believe in it, give money to it, and who intimidate and harm others to support it, count as terrorists or terrorist supporters?

Unless you are reading a different definition of terrorism, the answer must be *yes*.

Again, it is the goal and methodology of terrorism that we, and many others, stand so strongly against.

What I believe in, unequivocally, is that our democracy must be protected. MAGA stands out for its use of violence and intimidation to achieve its goals of controlling America. (If you are MAGA and this upsets you, please reread the definitions of terrorism again.) There are literally hundreds of MAGA serving prison sentences right now for acts that meet this definition. Per an article from the U.S. Department of Justice, as of January 4, 2024, more than a thousand rioters have been arrested for their actions on January 6, with 749 of the federal defendants receiving sentences for their crimes.[62]

I can't begin to list all the examples of this illegal activity (although I will list more later in this book), but here are just a few:

The January 6, 2021, Insurrection.

Death threats made on social media against people who have tried, or are trying, to prosecute or defame Donald Trump for his many alleged felonies. Felonies that he has been arrested for (strange how many law enforcement officers [LEOs] stand up for a brazen "alleged" career criminal.). And even death threats to election officials.[63]

Violent political intimidation, such as the surrounding of the "Biden bus" in Texas. And the inadequate response by the police there.[64]

Actions by MAGA members toward civilians that include intimidation, harassment, or violence, such as the previously discussed attack on Paul Pelosi by a hammer wielding MAGA supporter. We will go over more of these actions by MAGA in a later chapter and throughout the book.

Tribalism.

The action, or existence, of being organized in a tribe or tribes.

Tribalism is also used to describe situations where people are intensely loyal to their own group.[65]

Let's look at tribalism as it pertains to American politics.

We all tend to do this. We are loyal to our family, friends, and groups we belong to. But tribalism is more than this. It is an excessively intense loyalty to the group, a.k.a. the tribe, through actions (and inactions as well). There is no room for any group to be placed above the tribe, and loyalty is a requirement of continued membership.

For example, when I was an agent (especially for my last years since Trump and MAGA came into prominence in 2016), I endured ridicule and taunts of being "woke" or a "dirty lib." This would occur any time I spoke outside of a very narrow list of acceptable responses on any politically charged topic. Anyone who stepped outside of the Republican/MAGA Party line, on any topic, risked losing their status as a member of the tribe.

Once I started negatively talking about topics that were accepted by the MAGA tribe, or agreeing with views opposed, I was immediately ostracized. I noticed others, even when they disagreed with the MAGA viewpoint, remained silent so as not to lose their sense of belonging to the tribe. I wasn't alone, but those of us speaking out against MAGA were in the minority.

A disturbing number of our law enforcement and military members, both current and former, are in this "MAGA tribe." As a retired LEO, I still must qualify once a year to keep my credentials current. At both of my qualifications, some of the LEOs wore MAGA-associated items, or talked fondly of pro-MAGA topics.

IS MAGA A TERRORIST MOVEMENT?

About 15 percent of the 1,000 plus people arrested for the January 6 Insurrection have a background of military or law enforcement. For context, only 7 percent of the US population are military veterans, and less than 1 percent are police or sheriff patrol officers.[66]

MAGA is endemic in law enforcement in America and has effectively co-opted many of these officers. The unusually large percentage and number of LEOs and military in MAGA cannot be overlooked. I have personally seen large numbers of them working for the government during my tenure in law enforcement, and a disproportionately large number of January 6 rioters were current or former military and law enforcement.[67] Having been in both military and federal law enforcement, I can speak to the high levels of training that they have received, which includes: weapons and tactical training, other combat techniques, and years of practical real-world experience using that training. Because of this, these are especially dangerous individuals.

So what? Why should I care?

Well, people thought Hitler was a joke and would amount to nothing. The Afghanis thought the same about the Taliban in the beginning. And many Americans think the same way of Trump and his MAGA movement.

As Germans, Afghanis, and many other countries can attest: Once authoritarian regimes get control, it will be too little, too late, to stop them.

I am writing this book so others can understand just how real a threat to our democracy MAGA is. As I write this, Donald Trump is in the lead for the Republican presidential nomination. Keep in mind Trump and MAGA are inseparable entities. How can so many people still want a person with 91 felony charges to be president?

TERRORISM VS. TRIBALISM

According to a CBS News poll from November 2023, 100 percent of likely GOP primary voters who vote for Trump in the primary would go on to vote for him in the general election if he were the nominee. Of those voters who do not support Trump in the primary, 82 percent would still vote for him in the general election if he were the nominee.

The scariest part is, among likely GOP primary voters in this poll, 34 percent think better of him because he was indicted, and 54 percent say the indictments don't affect how they think of him. So, 88 percent of these Republicans don't care that he is an alleged hard-core career criminal. And more than a third think it's a plus![68]

I can tell you for a fact that if I had been charged, or even under investigation for, a *single* felony, my job and clearance would have been immediately suspended, or I would've been outright fired, and my clearance revoked. Why on earth is POTUS, the highest level of our executive branch, not required to pass the same clearance as our agents? Crazy, but they are not. They aren't held to the same standards as the rank and file. They don't have to pass the background checks and requirements that I did.[69]

We need that to change. As obvious as this sounds, *anyone* with access to classified material should have to pass a full background check, and maintain the standards, for that clearance. This is a *huge* problem with our system.

Imagine if I were trained to fly an aircraft, a 4-seat Cessna, but failed to pass my private pilot's license. Then they gave me a brief tutorial on flying a 777. I didn't pass training with that either, received no background check, and had no ongoing training standards...

Would you get on that plane with me as the pilot?

Take a seat and relax, that is our whole country in the air right now.

Unfortunately for us, you can even become POTUS as a convicted felon.[70] You may not be allowed to vote and can't be in the military or federal civilian service, but you can be in charge of them. Lunacy.

CHAPTER NINE
MAGA TERRORISM

BEFORE WE GET FURTHER into MAGA terrorism, we need to talk about the "War on Terror," a global, American-led military campaign launched following 9/11.[71]

Much like the "War on Crime"[72] or the "War on Drugs," this is an unwinnable war.

"But you said you would give us the steps to defeat them!"

I did, and I will. What I mean by unwinnable is that they can never be fully defeated. But individual organizations can be mitigated to a level where they have effectively lost.

In 1971, President Richard Nixon declared a "War on Drugs," but it had been ongoing for quite some time even before then. It is estimated the United States has spent over $1 trillion in the following fifty years on this war, but drugs are still here and are still a serious problem.[73]

IS MAGA A TERRORIST MOVEMENT?

Ditto the "War on Crime" and the "War on Terror." We can mitigate and decrease, through enforcement, these societal problems, but we can't eradicate them.

The best efforts of law enforcement can result in reduced crime, where people feel safe going out at night. We can deter and arrest members of gangs and drug dealers, but we will never get them all. And more will come.

But we *can* take on individual criminal organizations and dismantle them.

We can do that with MAGA. Just like other groups that use terrorism, such as the White supremacy movement, we can dismantle their individual organizations, arrest law breakers, and reduce them to a level where they don't pose a serious threat, much less a risk to taking over the entire government. And we can make sure they are seen for their despicable mindset, unworthy of inclusion in polite, law-abiding society.

But are Republicans, in general, supportive of White supremacy?

No and yes. No, many Republicans do not advocate directly for White supremacy. But that really doesn't matter. Why?

Because White supremacist groups openly and enthusiastically support MAGA. Richard Spencer, a White supremacist who runs the National Policy Institute, an alt right, White nationalist and White supremacist think tank,[74] said in an interview that Trump "seems to genuinely care about the historic American nation that is white people."[75] David Duke, a White nationalist and former Ku Klux Klan grand wizard, stated that voting against Trump "is really treason to your heritage."[76] These are just a couple of many examples of White supremacists supporting Trump.

Trump and MAGA support the goals of the White supremacy

movement with many of their actions and inactions. According to a Reuters/Ipsos poll from January 2024, Trump is leading in the polls to be the Republican presidential nominee with 49 percent. His closest rival, Nikki Haley, trails at just 12 percent.[77] So, in America's two-party system, that leaves only one logical conclusion: A vote for Republican, if Trump is the nominee, equals a vote for MAGA, which equals a vote for White supremacy. Inescapable logic.

So yes, Republicans who vote for Trump are supporting the White supremacy movement. That is what reason tells me. But again, you decide.

Talking more about terrorism, I wanted to add a little anecdote from my time in the army:

At the end of 1990, my unit was deployed for Operation Desert Storm. Our company motto was "first in, last out," a euphemism for MPs being the first there and last to leave. Not always true, but catchy. MP stands for "military police," but I quickly learned it also stood for "multi-purpose." One of the reasons I joined as an MP was because of its versatility—we were sent to most conflicts.

So, the war started, and we were deployed to the Middle East. After Saddam Hussein's Iraqi forces invaded Kuwait and seized their oil fields, we (America) went in to win the war, which we accomplished. But to "win" any war or engagement, the military has a concept. One I learned well as a new platoon leader years later. To win, you must have "clearly defined, achievable objectives." Once those are met, you win! Simple enough.

So is the war on MAGA unwinnable?

In Desert Storm, the objectives were to drive Iraq out of Kuwait and to effectively destroy its capacity to export warfare.[78] We did so.

You can always add new objectives and win them too. But

you can't destroy a concept. Socialism, communism, capitalism, fascism, Naziism, all alive and well today. So, we cannot have an unachievable objective like "destroy MAGA completely" or "eliminate all of MAGA." Those can be overreaching goals, but they are not objectives.

Defined, achievable objectives include keeping them from having a majority in Congress, or from having a MAGA POTUS or even a MAGA governor. Another thing I am in favor of is checking for MAGA affiliation in the recurrent government employee background checks. Unfortunately (at least at the time of my last one), they aren't checking for this. That needs to change.

If I had walked around my old field office talking about how America should be forced to follow Sharia law (which is a strictly enforced version of Islam) and about how extremist pseudo-Islam is the one true way because America, as it is now, is a failure; or if I had worn a patch on my jacket or a hat on my head showing my allegiance to terrorist groups that support this extremism, would I have kept my job?

I can tell you with certainty I would not have. Nor should I have.

Now, if I did the same *exact* things with MAGA as my terrorist group of choice:

If I had walked around the field office talking about how America should be forced to follow the doctrines of MAGA, and that POTUS and the current government are illegitimate, and we should be following the views of MAGA because America, as it is now, is a failure; or if I had worn a QAnon or Punisher patch on my jacket, or a "We the People Are Pissed Off" or "MAGA" hat on my head showing my allegiance to them? Would I have kept my job?

Yes. Yes, I would have.

I saw this very activity for *years* in my field office. No one was reprimanded or fired. I brought it up to management, multiple times, to no avail. Not only that, but other agents also brought up the threat of MAGA inside our agency. Also to no avail.

So, if they show support for the violent extremist MAGA movement, which has been proven to have attacked America, shouldn't they also meet the same fate? Well, if they did that, there would be thousands of job openings in the government right now!

Now you know where many of MAGA are today.

In your government. All branches. Both civilian and military.

Sweet dreams.

So, we discussed terrorism in general, but should MAGA be labeled a terrorist organization?

Let us look at the facts.

Over sixty terrorist groups have been designated by the US State Department as foreign terrorist organizations. We hear about them every day in the news. Hamas front and center at the moment. But so are Hizballah, ISIS, al-Qaeda, and al-Shabaab to name a few.[79]

What about domestic terrorists?

I found a long definition and explanation on the US Department of the Treasury website. It says that domestic terrorism involves activities that are dangerous to people; are illegal at the state or federal level; appear to be intended to coerce or intimidate a civilian population, or to affect the conduct of the government by mass destruction, assassination, or kidnapping; and primarily occur in the jurisdiction of the United States.[80]

Do people in America who support MAGA's stated goals meet this definition? Do they use intimidation and threats of harm, or actual harm, to achieve their political goals? Are these activities dangerous to human life and in violation of federal or state laws? Well, an article from ABC News highlighted over fifty cases involving threats, violence, and alleged assaults directly linked to Trump through court documents and police statements. And these are just the ones where Trump was mentioned. How many more cases are there?[81]

Let's look at the leader of the MAGA movement, former president Donald Trump. He has been arrested and charged with over 90 felonies. He has pleaded not guilty to all of them:

- 4 charges for the January 6 Insurrection case
- 40 charges for the classified documents case in Florida
- 34 charges for the business fraud case in New York
- 13 charges for the Georgia 2020 election interference case[82]

Several of these felonies are related not only to him, but also to his many accomplices for attempting to overthrow the US government. As well as for violating the Constitution and even fomenting an insurrection. Not to mention the possession and sharing of classified documents with those without a need to know or the proper clearance.[83]

In the performance of my federal career, both civilian and military, I dealt with classified information. I have never, and will never, share what I know now that I am a regular citizen. Maybe Trump would have forty less felony charges if he realized he now has as much reason to personally possess, or talk about, classified documents as I do—none.

As we have already discussed, over a thousand people have been charged for their involvement in the January 6 Insurrection, with hundreds already serving lengthy sentences for their crimes.

The nexus is clear. The activities of these MAGA supporters have a common theme—to force political change with illegal intimidation, coercion, and force.

After reviewing the facts, yes, in my opinion, I think MAGA is a domestic terrorist organization (DTO).

But it isn't.

Wait, what?!

According to the CIA's database, MAGA has not been declared an official terrorist organization.[84]

The attack on the Capitol on January 6 was denounced as an act of domestic terrorism by the White House, the FBI, and the Department of Justice (DOJ).[85] But the US government, as I write this in 2024, has still not labeled MAGA a DTO. Nor have prosecutors successfully brought forth charges specifically with the enhancement (harsher sentencing penalty) for terrorism. The terrorism-related language now includes federal criminal offenses that use coercion or intimidation to influence, affect, or retaliate against the government or its conduct.[86]

Does this sound like anything that those who have been charged have done? How about the actions of the many people who haven't been charged? The surrounding of a "Biden bus" or the social media attacks and death threats to politicians or citizens who they disagree with? If this were a foreign terrorist organization doing these actions, would they be allowed to continue?

Not only has MAGA not been charged with terrorism, but the federal and state governments won't even recognize them as a terrorist group. Is it because literally millions of Americans identify with and support MAGA terrorism? It does seem that way ...

This is why we should all be very concerned.

CHAPTER TEN
GOVERNMENT IN ACTION

Government Inaction

Well, now for the elephant in the room—let's talk about the US government. How is the government both part of the problem *and* part of the solution? Let's delve ...

We all know what action is, but its brother, inaction, is a lack of action where some is appropriate or expected. This can fall under a related term: nonfeasance. Nonfeasance is a failure to act, especially a failure to do what ought to be done. This can be a criminal or civil violation if the person committing it had a legal responsibility to act.[87]

So, the US government has a mandate to protect us and our constitutional rights. It also has an obligation to find and prosecute those who break our laws. So, some action is expected and appropriate.

But how does that mandate work if the government itself has ("alleged") criminals in charge? It still does, but less well. It had to wait to investigate and charge a sitting president, per DOJ policy.[88] Constitutional protections suddenly started only applying to some people, not all.

Examples? Protections for LGBTQ+ and women were successfully attacked by the Trump administration.[89] Republicans have been trying to gut the Voting Rights Act so that many minorities will not have equal access to voting.[90] The sources I picked show long lists of the actions taken to achieve these goals.

What was the overwhelming response by the Republican Party? That it wasn't a big deal.

The GOP fought against the January 6 committee by blocking the creation of a bipartisan panel to investigate the attack on the Capitol.[91]

Senate Republicans blocked a bill that would combat domestic terrorism.[92]

The GOP fought against saying Donald Trump was responsible in any way for the insurrection, to include defending him when it was clear he was guilty during impeachments (plural). In fact, the retaliation against the ten Republicans who did the right thing and voted to impeach Trump has led to only two of them advancing to the general election. Four didn't seek reelection and four lost their primaries. MAGA has a history of going after anyone that works against them or their undisputed leader, Donald Trump.[93]

Republican Congress members vowed to object to the Electoral College votes in "disputed states" for the 2020 presidential election, in violation of the Twelfth Amendment. The wording in the Twelfth Amendment is clear—Congress's only job is to count the Electoral votes cast by each state. Not to interpret or debate, just count and enter the results into the record. Thankfully, cooler heads prevailed and, following the riot at the Capitol, the vote was later counted and certified properly.[94] Our government held against tyranny.

This time.

On the flip side, the DOJ has been aggressively prosecuting January 6 criminals, but only *after* Trump left office. Did they go after the Oath Keepers and Proud Boys before the attack? Did they have undercover agents infiltrating these terrorist groups? Probably not, because no one dared to label them that. Even now there is no federal statute for domestic terrorism. MAGA, Proud Boys, Oath Keepers, or the neo-Nazi groups such as the National Socialist Movement or Atomwaffen Division are not officially terrorist organizations, a designation that would make them legitimate terror groups where the government could seize assets (asset forfeiture) and criminally charge members for any "material support of terrorism."[95]

So, I commend everyone in government who is helping to bring these criminals to justice. It is a hard job made harder by our inefficient classification apparatus.

Does MAGA agree with making themselves or their supporters, such as the Proud Boys, official domestic terrorist groups?

I am very curious to see MAGA supporters writing in, trying to show how the DOJ, the FBI, and the Department of Homeland Security (DHS) have only been "weaponized" against them. (We will talk about the "Weaponization of the Federal Government" in the next chapter.)

That term has only, to my knowledge, been used to describe these agencies "going after" criminals with political connections. Specifically, Republicans take umbrage with criminal probes of

IS MAGA A TERRORIST MOVEMENT?

Donald Trump and his MAGA supporters. They have no problem with these "weapons" being aimed at Democrats …

According to an article in *The Hill*, one thing that is a common refrain for MAGA is the concept of "projection." This is where they attribute their own illicit motivations onto their opponents. So far, "the weaponization of the federal government" subcommittee in the House has found very little evidence of the federal government being weaponized by Democrats.[96] Maybe if it wasn't, in my opinion, a Republican controlled sham (and by itself, a perfect example of weaponizing the government), it would take a hard look at what happened from, oh I don't know, maybe 2017–2021? Plenty of attempts to weaponize the federal government took place during the Trump administration. In fact, a large part of this book is about those actions …

Perhaps this adversarial relationship has more to do with criminals not liking law enforcement? If MAGA can prove that our federal law enforcement is busy protecting criminals, especially only Democrats, I would love to see it!

So, if Republicans support MAGA, and MAGA supports Trump …

Is voting Republican, as the Party is today, a vote to support MAGA and Trump? I would argue, yes.

I think Rep. Liz Cheney (R-WY) understood this and lost her primary in August 2022 against her Donald Trump backed challenger for daring to vote to impeach Trump, and for her role on the January 6 committee. MAGA terrorism isn't just *in* the government now, it is also being directed *at* members of the government.[97]

Shout out to Liz Cheney, you are a true patriot. Even if I don't agree with many of your conservative viewpoints, you were there for our country when it counted. Thank you!

GOVERNMENT IN ACTION

When we elected Donald Trump in 2016 (yes, Donald Trump, just like Joe Biden in 2020, was duly elected), we put the monster in charge of the machine. As he broke down (or tried to break down) anything that stood in his way of power, this led to some unusual activity in the government. When it became clear he had lost the election in 2020, he did not concede power—unlike every other American president in modern history. That's OK. No law required it.

What the law *did* require was for him to lawfully relinquish that power on Inauguration Day (January 20, 2021) and to not break the law trying to subvert the election illegally.

A coup d'état, or coup for short, is an attempt to overthrow or alter an existing government, usually by a small group and especially if they use force to do it. A self-coup is when a leader, who was put in power legally, tries to stay in power using illegal methods.[98]

I can think of no more accurate of an example of self-coup than Donald Trump and his supporters before, during, and after the 2020 presidential election.

One of MAGA's claims is that Joe Biden didn't receive anywhere near the votes "they" say he did. I had many, um, "interesting" debates about this with MAGA when I was a Fed.

Even a family member said to me, "Do you really think over 80 million people voted for Joe Biden?"

I told him I did not. I think most of those votes, now that America has been forced into a two-party system, were not for Joe Biden, but *against* Donald Trump. President Biden is a fine president, especially considering what he has accomplished working with an adversarial GOP. That aside, I would have voted for almost anyone—or even a squirrel—over voting for Trump.

The fact is that both broke the record for the highest number of votes ever received in a presidential election. Trump received more votes than any sitting president, ever, with over 74 million votes. Unfortunately for him and MAGA, and fortunately for everyone else, Biden got over 81 million.[99]

I am very glad Trump lost. I am not exaggerating when I say that our liberal democracy will start to end the day he takes office again. Especially now.

If the "Teflon Don" can beat 91 felony counts and win the presidency again, he and his supporters can easily make short work of the checks and balances in our government to solidify their power forevermore.

CHAPTER ELEVEN
MAGA IN THE HOUSE

REP. MIKE JOHNSON. He gets his own chapter for what a true MAGA representative he is.

So, who is he? He is our new Speaker of the House.

How did that happen? Well, unlike the fifteen times it took to get Rep. Kevin McCarthy (R-CA) into the Speakership, Mike Johnson (R-LA) was voted in unanimously by his party on the first vote. He was welcomed by the "far right," which, along with its MAGA voting base, now effectively controls the Republican Party.[100]

Yes, every Republican in the House voted for him, which says something very important when you look at his pro-MAGA background.

He is well known for his pseudo-Christian viewpoint. He worked for the evangelical Christian legal group Alliance Defense Fund (ADF), which is now known as the Alliance Defending Freedom. As they are a pro-life organization, we can assume they do not defend your freedom of choice. So, they are defending *their* freedom, not necessarily *your* freedom. ADF has also worked hard against the rights of LGBTQ+ groups for years.[101]

According to an article from ABC News, Johnson is also a constitutional lawyer who argued that the 2020 election was fraudulent in an attempt to keep Donald Trump in power.[102] I guess just because you know constitutional law doesn't mean you choose to follow it.

He also sits on the Judiciary committee (and chairs a subcommittee on the Constitution), the Armed Services Committee,[103] and this one is scary …

He sits on the newly created select committee on "Weaponization of the Federal Government."[104]

Think about that. A Trump-supporting Republican, who now leads the House of Representatives, on a committee with the laughable idea that enforcing our laws is now being "weaponized." But *only* when it is prosecuting MAGA or Republican targets. Totally appropriate as a "weapon" when they use the exact same methods to investigate Democrats. Are you sick of their hypocrisy?

So, when pseudo-Christians and MAGA call those who disagree with them "woke," keep in mind what their "insult" really means. In their opinion, woke means people who care about racism, sexism, homophobia, and not having to follow the tyrannical application of a hard-right "fire and brimstone" version of the Bible that takes away our freedoms instead of protecting them.

What is the opposite of "woke"? Asleep.

Asleep is what you must be to not realize authoritarian government will never be in your favor unless you are part of the top 1 percent in the country. Also, if you want to alienate and anger literally everyone who isn't a straight, White, pseudo-Christian man, you are, I hope, still asleep.

OK, back to our resident, third-in-succession-to-be-POTUS, pseudo-Christian Johnson. He stated, "There is clearly no 'right to sodomy' in the Constitution." He is wrong.

In *Lawrence v. Texas*, the Supreme Court of the United States held that "a Texas law criminalizing consensual, sexual conduct between individuals of the same sex violates the Due Process Clause of the Fourteenth Amendment." Per Justice Anthony Kennedy, "When homosexual conduct is made criminal by the law of the State, that declaration in and of itself is an invitation to subject homosexual persons to discrimination both in the public and in the private spheres."[105]

So, for a constitutional lawyer, he sure doesn't know the Constitution very well.

Do you know what else is in the Constitution?

The very First Amendment: "Congress shall make no law respecting an establishment of religion, or prohibiting the free exercise thereof; or abridging the freedom of speech, or of the press, or the right of the people peaceably to assemble, and to petition the government for a redress of grievances."

The first ten amendments were ratified effective December 15, 1791. What that means, in simple terms, is that these are some of the most important rights we have—and they have been for over 232 years.

Where am I going with this? Well, it seems to me that these pseudo-Christians are trying to enshrine their version of the Bible into law. That is what groups like the ADF are about, trying to put into secular law the religious dogma of their beliefs. That directly violates the First Amendment: "Congress shall make no law respecting an establishment of religion."

Let's apply logic again and flip the script to see if what they believe about passing religious dogma into law is OK.

If Mr. Johnson was an extremist pseudo-Muslim in charge of the House of Representatives with a 100 percent approval rating from the Democrats, do you think Republicans would be OK with that? How about when he makes it clear he will support extremist pseudo-Muslim views and get them passed into law whether Republicans, or pseudo-Christians, complained about it or not? Is passing laws to specifically support the tenets of a religion not against the Constitution? Is it only if they pass the whole religion into law at once? Since Mike Johnson is a constitutional lawyer, he knows the real answer, but will never say it. I argue that what he is doing *is* unconstitutional and it must be fought by any true American.

My mother is a Christian and I was raised in this faith as a child. She is horrified when she is wrongly associated with extremist pseudo-Christians. MAGA has co-opted her religion as well.

She is horrified for the same reason millions of Muslims are horrified when they are misassociated with extremist pseudo-Muslims who want to enforce Sharia law.

The extremists of *any* religion are a threat to our freedom.

In the early 2000s Islamophobia was rampant. Some people were attacking anyone who looked Muslim. Were the victims of their violence the ones who attacked us or supported the terrorists of 9/11? Of course not.[106]

My mom and other Christians aren't supporting MAGA just because the pseudo-Christians do any more than those innocent Muslims were supporting pseudo-Muslims.

I learned early on in my career to look for the indicators of criminality and terrorism. It isn't your religion or race that makes you a criminal. It's the desire to trample on other people's rights to live peaceably and to do it in an illegal way. Only a tiny number of people of any religion or race are "bad" people. They are easy to spot. They are the extremists.

I know many people of all religious backgrounds, to include atheists and agnostics. We all want freedom of, but more importantly freedom *from*, religion. No law should be passed abridging our freedom when we are not hurting others.

As I said earlier, Rep. Johnson has received high praise and 100 percent support from all Republicans in the House. Scary times.

CHAPTER TWELVE
MORALITY POLICE

LET'S TALK ABOUT THE DIFFERENCES between morality enforcement versus law enforcement. Today I read an article about the murder of a teenager in Iran. She was beaten (allegedly—again eye roll) by morality police, went into a coma, and then died.

Another young woman, Mahsa Amini, just twenty-two years old, was murdered for the same "offense" in Iran in 2022. Iranian authorities say she suffered a heart attack in police custody.[107] Pretty normal for a twenty-two-year-old to have a heart attack, no?

Why was she killed? Because she wasn't wearing her headscarf, called a hijab, correctly and dared to get into an altercation with the Iranian "morality police."

OK, if you are not in Iran, why should you care?

Well, we know what law enforcement is. It is, quite simply, the enforcement of a nation's, state's, or local government's laws.

IS MAGA A TERRORIST MOVEMENT?

Presumably, at least in the United States, these are laws by the people, and for the people, who live there.

I am proud of my work for law enforcement over the course of my career. But that is because (for now) we, in America, live in a liberal democracy. I would not have been a police officer in Iran. I would have been a freedom fighter against the regime.

So, from police to criminal. Why? Because the laws we live under must be just. It doesn't matter if our rights are taken away by religious fatwa, commandment, or simply by an authoritarian government. They are gone just the same.

As citizens of the United States, we want to know that our law enforcement is doing their absolute best to protect our rights and enforce the law. Do we want "morality police" like in Iran? MAGA does. How can I say this? Let's look at something MAGA pushes for that is clearly about morality enforcement and not protection:

Transgender people using a public bathroom. Clearly a dangerous crime.

Before we start, a little personal background. As an undercover agent in Europe years ago (waiting for a flight home, not actively working), I was using a urinal. In the men's bathroom. A cleaning woman came up to the urinal next to mine to clean it. She wasn't embarrassed, and neither was I. It was normal there. It's just a bathroom.

Fast-forward a bit and North Carolina had just passed a bill, HB2 (the "bathroom bill"). This new law made it illegal to use, or be in, a public restroom that does not match the gender you were assigned at birth. This was passed on March 23, 2016, during Donald Trump's presidential campaign.[108]

Some of my MAGA coworkers loved this new law and asked me

if I had an issue with it. A classic "Own the Libs" moment. (This is an example of the hostile environment I worked in.)

I said I did have a problem with it. They said it was needed to protect kids from transgenders using the bathroom. There is a myth, perpetuated by the conservative right, that transgender people are pedophiles and sexual predators. As if there aren't plenty of non-transgender versions of those. OK, so let's look at some facts before we continue with the story. According to an article in Slate, "The Real Reason the Religious Right Opposes Trans Equality. (It Isn't Bathroom Predators.)," the religious right is not highly concerned about their safety in bathrooms; they are just anti-LGBTQ+.[109]

How many people have been attacked *by* transgender people in restrooms?

According to an article in MIC titled, "Statistics Show Exactly How Many Times Trans People Have Attacked You in Bathrooms," we find accurate facts instead of the unsubstantiated right-wing fear of LGBTQ+ "predator attacks." In 2015, spokespersons for the Transgender Law Center, the Human Rights Campaign, and the American Civil Liberties Union said that there was no statistical evidence of violence to warrant the many states that were trying to pass bills to limit bathroom use by transgenders.

So, in other words, zero. Not a single documented case of violence perpetrated by a transgender person in a bathroom. How about *against* a transgender person in a bathroom?

According to that same 2015 National Transgender Discrimination Survey report, roughly 70 percent of transgender people have reported being denied entrance, assaulted, or harassed while trying to use the restroom.[110]

70 percent vs. 0 percent

So, the lie that we need protection from transgender predators going into our bathrooms is just that. A lie.

So what, what do I care? I wasn't scared of that anyway.

Do you know who *is* scared to use a public restroom? Transgender people. And whether MAGA likes it or not, transgender people in America have two things in common with everyone else—they are Americans and they are protected by the Constitution. In other words, MAGA is needlessly attacking their right to free movement and needlessly discriminating against them. MAGA still doesn't care? Time for my answer on what I would do …

I responded that you are many times more likely to be assaulted *as* a transgender person than *by* a transgender person. Turns out I was wrong. It should have been "no chance of being attacked by a transgender."

So, by 2024, has there been a case? I don't know. But I am sure even if there has, it is minuscule compared to the thousands of transgender people that have been attacked.

I asked them if this law would apply if I walked into the women's restroom. They said yes. So I asked, what if I looked like I did now, but was a transgender man, should I still be in there?

How about if I see a man bringing a female child (presumably their daughter) into the men's room?

Should I arrest them both? According to the law, I should. Her for being there, and him for contributing to the delinquency of a minor, or even child abuse (since it is so dangerous to be in the "wrong" bathroom).

Stupid MAGA silence ensues …

Am I being a bit mean, saying they are stupid? Turns out I am just using the right vocabulary. Stupid is the correct term for MAGA.

Ignorance is just having a lack of information or knowledge about something.[111] Stupid is lacking intelligence or reason.[112]

So, stupid it is.

There is no fundamental difference between the hijab dress code enforcement law in Iran and the bathroom laws passed in America. It is an attack on a minority group that is meant to open the floodgate to more restrictive laws to follow. In Iran it is to put women "in their place." Here in America, it is to put LGBTQ+ "in their place."

Both practices are vile and need to be stopped.

It's obvious what MAGA truly wants:

Based on the laws that have been passed and introduced in various states, in my opinion, MAGA's goal is not for transgender people to be forced out of their bathrooms. It is for them to be forced out of their communities, and out of MAGA's new "great" America. Or better yet, to not exist at all.

CHAPTER THIRTEEN
FASCISM

I HAVE HEARD THE WORD "fascist" thrown around when referring to people in MAGA or on the extreme right. Is this the correct term?

A lot of times, it is.

But just as I have heard the term "racist" sometimes used incorrectly, I have also heard this term used incorrectly.

So, you know me at this point, here is how we describe fascism:

Fascism is a governmental system led by a dictator. That government has complete power and forcibly suppresses any form of criticism or opposition. It emphasizes and demands an aggressive nationalism and is often racist. Fascism is also the methodology or principles of fomenting fascism.[113]

Wow. It is disconcerting to even write these words.

Does this sound like what MAGA wants? Does it resonate in the "America First" policies of MAGA? Even if you are MAGA and reading this, can you honestly say that political action by Trump and the GOP was not guided by these principles to achieve its objectives? Do they want undisputed and complete control of the entire government, with a powerful "president" in charge?

I have had conversations with MAGA about this topic. I asked them if they could have complete control of the branches of government, even if it meant there would be no more effective resistance by Democrats, would they support that?

Almost all of them said yes. I, on the other hand, would not. Even if it were Democrats having complete control, that is against democracy and for tyranny.

Our first president, George Washington, was purported to have been offered kingship over America after the Revolutionary War. He would not even entertain the notion.[114]

Do you think Trump would voluntarily relinquish almost absolute power like Washington did? Or would he take the title and position of king, you know, for the good of the country?

So, back to the question: Is MAGA fascist? You can decide for yourself … it sure looks that way to me.

CHAPTER FOURTEEN
FACT VS. FICTION

BEFORE WE START, let's define some things. We will use Dictionary.com for our definitions:

What is a "fact"?

"That which actually exists or is the case; reality or truth: something known to exist or to have happened."

What is "fiction"?

"Something feigned, invented, or imagined; a made-up story."[115]

One of the things many MAGA supporters like to use to counter any argument that they deem wrong is to question the validity of everything you say to them. Not a bad thing; it's just the intent I find worrisome. Their intent is not to learn, but just to "win" their argument. An excellent article by Next Big Idea Club, "Facts Don't Change People's Minds. Here's What Does," covers the confirmation bias that allows for people to hold onto beliefs that are verifiably false. It explains that a person's response to being shown irrefutable proof that their belief is not correct is not usually to change their beliefs, but instead to attack the person saying it. To accept the truth would require change on their part.[116] If their belief is core to their identity and acceptance by a peer group (such as the MAGA cult), they will fight the truth rather than accept it. If they accept something demonstrably true that refutes any of the ideals and beliefs of MAGA, they will be ostracized from the tribe.

If someone using factual information can convince me that I am wrong, I am open to it. It has happened before.

I believed that there was an element of creationism, not just evolution, in how life on earth evolved. I am not embarrassed to say it. I would be embarrassed to learn something new and not change my way of thinking.

As adults, I was talking with a childhood friend. He tried to convince me that evolution was real, and creationism was not. I was still ignorant—you could even say I was being stupid—and was not convinced.

Later, after personally researching the facts, I concluded that a combined millennia of academic research by scientists were (shocker, I know) accurate.

Evolution is real (fact), creationism is not (fiction). Or at least there is no actual physical proof of creationism.

This will make some—OK a lot—of people angry. That is not my intent.

For example, let's use my mom again.

She is a great woman. She is kind to everyone, and she looks forward to Heaven. I am not taking that from her. Or anyone else. It is a belief, a "faith," that there will be a reward in the afterlife for being a good person. I don't see anything wrong with that. It helps her treat others the way she would want to be treated (do unto others as you would have them do unto you). It helps her to have a goal (eternity in Heaven). She likes to spend time with her fellow church members, and this makes her happy. She doesn't seek to disparage, harm, or have prejudice against others. She is a true Christian.

Why do I mention this?

Because the pseudo-Christians who support MAGA do not believe in facts. How can I prove this to be a true statement? Here are some examples:

The First Amendment prohibits the establishment of religion into secular law. If you are a patriot, you support the Constitution. MAGA considers themselves consummate patriots. Patriots that want to establish laws to support their religious beliefs. Laws that violate the First Amendment. Hmm …

MAGA says transgender bathroom attacks are a major problem. Even though evidence of any attacks are hard to even find, much less common occurrences.

The concept of treating others as you would like to be treated, which is in the Bible, is not being followed by MAGA pseudo-Christians. Their bigotry and hate are in the open for the world to see.

Remember why we use pseudo-Christian and pseudo-Muslim (or pseudo-religion) for this book. It is because most religious people do not give in to supporting hate to make their religion more powerful. It is the extremists among them that do.

IS MAGA A TERRORIST MOVEMENT?

The whole concept of these MAGA pseudo-Christians and their actions defies logic. We are, according to many religions, supposed to be here only to experience and learn before the afterlife. *Not* to enforce our religion or aspects of our religious beliefs on others. How do I know this? Because Jesus says so:

According to the King James Version (KJV) Bible:

Jesus on judging others: Matthew 7:2
"For with what judgment ye judge, ye shall be judged: and with what measure ye mete, it shall be measured to you again."[117]

Jesus on showing kindness to others: John 13:5

"After that he poureth water into a bason, and began to wash the disciples' feet, and to wipe them with the towel wherewith he was girded."[118]

He taught others to love each other, as brothers and sisters. In short, to be kind.

MAGA, are you being kind to others who are not like you? It is not too late to change your ways.

MAGA has made it clear. They support bigotry, sexism against women (misogyny), and racism. MAGA has also made clear they are OK with using (or supporting or acquiescing to) terrorism to accomplish their goal of political power. Pretty sure Jesus would not approve. Not at all. If your God is all powerful, then let me make it clear:

He, She, or It, does not need your help. Not even a little.

There are no physical, tangible things or factual events that prove that God is real at all. The whole premise is faith.

Faith is trust or confidence in a person or thing, or a belief that is not based on proof.[119]

Faith is accepting something is true, even when there is no physical proof, or there is proof to the contrary.

Such as faith that the election was stolen; that your leader isn't a career criminal; or that Jesus supports your racist, misogynistic, bigoted, and hateful ways. That is faith.

Evil faith, but it is faith.

But don't look up if you are a pseudo-Christian who believes in this. Look down.

Who do you think wants us at each other's throats? Jesus? Unlikely.

One of the arguments I heard from MAGA was that climate change isn't real. Makes sense. Election deniers and climate deniers both face the same dilemma— their beliefs are not based on fact. In reality, the facts 100 percent refute their claims. Yet they still believe. Why? Because you can't force a conversion; it must come of their own free will. But you can have faith and share it with others without needing a shred of proof.

Another conversation I had with MAGA was about "conversion therapy."

According to an article from the American Medical Association, conversion therapy is the practice of seeking to "convert" LGBTQ+ people to the sexual orientation or gender/expression traditionally associated with their assigned sex at birth. Also known as reparative therapy or sexual orientation change efforts (SOCE). Practitioners believe that any gender identity or sexual orientation other than cisgender and heterosexual is sinful, deviant, and unnatural. (The term cisgender is denoting or relating to a person whose gender identity corresponds with the sex registered for them at birth; not transgender.)[120]

So, a group of us were sitting around talking while we worked. While I can't reproduce the conversation word for word (unauthorized recording in our office was grounds for severe disciplinary action), I can provide a detailed overview that clearly expresses the sentiments of those involved.

Conversion therapy came up and I laughed about it. One of the MAGA supporters was offended. He said conversion therapy works and that he had personally seen its success with a "previously gay" male member of his church. Hmm …

The gauntlet was thrown.

I asked, rhetorically, if he really believed that. He answered he did. So, I offered him a logic loop to disprove his ridiculous idea.

Do you notice how few LQBTQ+ people live in countries where they have punishing laws against it? Do you think they just have less of them, or that they changed their ways? Or did their "therapy" only change their behavior in public because of the threat of persecution? Did they really "stop being gay"?

I asked him a hypothetical. It went something like this:

> "If you were gay and went through conversion therapy because you lived in a place that persecuted you through laws or excommunication from your tribe, would it work? Would you stop being gay and only be heterosexual?"

"Yes, I would," he responded.

"OK then, if we lived where it was a stoning offense to be heterosexual, and I put you through conversion therapy to be gay, would you be gay?"

"NO!" (Said with a look of disgust, I might add. That I *do* remember exactly.)

So, if you find women attractive, as a man, I can't make your desires change and just like men instead?

"NO."

"Then what on earth makes you think a gay man can be converted any more than a straight man could be?"

A lot of laughing from some of the 100+ IQ folks. Angry glares from many of the MAGA ones.

My point isn't about "winning" a debate. If we win or lose, it doesn't change facts or reality in any way.

Trump won the election in 2016. Fact.

Biden won, and Trump lost, in 2020. Fact.

It was thousands of MAGA that attacked the Capitol on January 6. Fact.

The January 6 attack on the US Capitol was an insurrection. Fact.

MAGA attacked the Capitol of their own free will and are accountable for those actions in a court of law. Those arrested and convicted are not "hostages" as, according to an article in the Iowa Capitol Dispatch, Trump referred to them in a campaign speech in Iowa on the third anniversary of the insurrection.[121] They are convicted criminals. Fact.

MAGA's use of intimidation, coercion, and harm to achieve political objectives against the civilian population and our government meets the criteria in the definition of terrorism. Fact.

MAGA's intolerant and obstinate devotion to its own opinions and prejudices that include enforcing sexism, religious intolerance, sexual orientation intolerance, and racism are not only bigotry, but unconstitutional. We have already discussed the ways in which their attempts to violate several amendments are not in line with the Constitution as it exists today. Fact.

Attacking your fellow Americans, just because they have beliefs that are different from yours, is not only illegal but un-American. The article we talked about earlier, "'No Blame? ABC News finds 54 cases invoking 'Trump' in connection with violence, threats, alleged assaults," outlined these assaults in detail. So, again, Fact.

According to the Twelfth Amendment of the Constitution:

Stopping the ratification of votes for POTUS on January 6 (Congress resumed later) is a direct violation of the Twelfth Amendment of the Constitution. Anyone who supported the insurrection on January 6 (or worse, who were directly involved) or gave "aid and comfort" to those who committed the act were in violation of the Constitution. Fact.

Supporting MAGA and the rioters; fighting against investigations of January 6; voting not to impeach Trump over January 6; condoning the attack on the Capitol and its police officers, through word and deed. These are examples of the inconsistencies with the Republicans' key claim of supporting "law and order." Fact.

There are many, many more examples of facts that prove MAGA's beliefs and worldview of American "patriotism" are not grounded in the reality of their actions. These examples just scratch the surface of their giant ball of lies and false idealism.

CHAPTER FIFTEEN
GOP: THE PARTY OF LAW AND ORDER

ONE OF THE PRINCIPLES OF THE GOP (Grand Old Party, a.k.a. the Republican Party) is that it has always prided itself on being the party that supports law enforcement officers and is strict on supporting the enforcement of our laws.

To wit, here is an excerpt from the Republican National Convention titled "Republican Platform 2016":

> "The next president must restore the public's trust in law enforcement and civil order by first adhering to the rule of law himself. Additionally, the next president must not sow seeds of division and distrust between the police and the people they have sworn to serve and protect. The Republican Party, a party of law and order, must make clear in words and action that every human life matters."[122]

So, how did they do? That next president they were referring to? Yup, that was Donald Trump.

Prior to 2016, I had appreciated the Republican Party's resolve to support law and order.

A funny thing happened over time though …

The GOP went from supporting law and order during a riot (about a minority who was killed), to defending an insurrection against police officers and the nation's Capitol (when it was MAGA who was involved). Many MAGA I spoke with tried to blame Antifa for the provocation of the January 6 riot.

OK then. I guess I am going to be permanently off their Christmas list, but that is OK. I pointed out that Antifa is short for "Anti-FASCISM." So, the exact opposite of what Trump and MAGA are trying to accomplish. As I have already shown you in this book, MAGA is a terrorist movement and MAGA is fascist.

So, why would Antifa be involved on January 6?

They wouldn't.

I am not saying every aspect of how Antifa acts is sunshine and rainbows, but the MAGA rioters were quite successful looking bad on their own. Over a thousand people being charged criminally and hundreds in prison will attest to this. Most with clear ties to MAGA. There was no need to make them look like violent insurrectionists. They did that just fine on their own!

Maybe Antifa wanted a fascist, racist leader to stay in power? Especially one like Donald Trump. Yes, that would certainly be a *top* priority for Antifa …

CHAPTER SIXTEEN
THE END JUSTIFIES THE MEANS

AS I HAVE ALREADY ALLUDED TO, the end does *not* justify the means.

It never has and it never will.

I am a patriot. Not at the level of George Washington, or of Martin Luther King, or of countless others who have sacrificed more, but a patriot nonetheless.

I take my oath to defend the Constitution and the rights of everyday Americans seriously. I am no longer on duty to do so, but my oath didn't say "… until you stop working for the government." It is a part of who I am, as a person.

We are taking a risk, you and I, by engaging the enemy. We are only "safe" if we remain silent and uninvolved.

If I could wave a magic wand and make MAGA disappear forever, I would. But would we be OK with a fascist or authoritarian government, even one ruled by Democrats, in order to stop them?

IS MAGA A TERRORIST MOVEMENT?

Absolutely not.

The quick and easy way to tell if something is anti-American is simple. Just ask yourself some basic questions. Or more appropriately, let MAGA answer these questions.

Does it violate the Constitution?

Does it unnecessarily limit our own or others' rights, if those rights are not putting others into harm's way?

Are you helping violate others with #1 or #2 above?

The way to tell if the philosophy of "the end justifies the means," at least for liberal American democracy, is anti-American is also simple:

Is the end result worth destroying the protections of our rights and the Constitution?

Is the end result worth establishing a fascist or authoritarian government?

If the laws you want implemented were reworded to apply to you as the harmed party, instead of whatever group you are limiting/harming, would you still support them?

Pretty straightforward stuff. The stuff of intellectual discussions to be sure. Doesn't go well with MAGA, I can tell you. Anytime someone uses the "I know you are, but what am I?" defense, you know you've got them in a corner. They simply have no defense to your argument and are forced to deflect.

I have had MAGA supporters say to me, "What about Biden?" or "Why not lock up Hillary over her emails?" when I mentioned Trump's latest wrongdoing.

I asked them if one person committed a felony, and then another person did, would you want them both in jail? Even if one was a Republican and the other was a Democrat?

In their defense, most of them did say yes. But when I asked how they felt about a (ahem, "alleged") career criminal being commander-in-chief of the United States again, they said that was OK. Which leads me to the chapter that is the biggest (or should I say "BIGLY-IST") threat to our freedom ...

CHAPTER SEVENTEEN
IS TRUMP A TRAITOR?

SO, I AM DARING TO ASK THE QUESTION: Is Donald Trump a traitor? What proof is there? Does he meet the definition of being a traitor? This is a big deal, to say the least. We learn by researching things, not just taking one person's word for something. Accusing someone is easy. MAGA does it all the time. Showing that person did something wrong takes a lot more work. So, looking at the facts and letting you decide makes more sense.

Well, let's look, shall we?

I have heard the term "traitor" thrown around inaccurately as much as I have heard "fascist" and "racist" being used incorrectly.

A traitor is a person who betrays a cause, another person, or any trust. It is also describing a person who commits treason by betraying their country.[123]

So, does Donald Trump meet these parameters?

Looking at the first part of being a traitor, let's think back to Chapter Seven's "Oath of Office."

Does telling a crowd, as POTUS did, to "fight like hell" or "you're not going to have a country anymore" sound like a betrayal of this oath?[124] Does it betray the trust that was given to him when he became president and took his oath of office?

Does the fact that he did it within walking distance to the Capitol, on the day they were ratifying the vote he lost, mean anything?

How about if the stopping of the vote ratification directly violated the Twelfth Amendment of the Constitution?

Under federal law 18 USC section 2101, inciting a riot means to "organize, promote, encourage, participate in, or carry on a riot." This includes "urging or instigating other persons to riot."[125]

Under the Twelfth Amendment, Congress is to ratify the vote for POTUS and VPOTUS. Interfering with that is unconstitutional and illegal. That was what happened on January 6, 2021. Did he incite a riot to stop the ratification of the vote (to replace himself as president)? Does that meet the criteria of a self-coup also?

So, did he betray the trust of his oath and of his country?

What about his claims that he is protected by the First Amendment of free speech?

Let's look at the two legal prongs that constitute incitement of imminent lawless action based on *Brandenburg v. Ohio* (known as the Brandenburg test):

Advocacy of force or criminal activity does not receive First Amendment protections if (1) the advocacy is directed to inciting or producing imminent lawless action, and (2) is likely to incite or produce such action.[126]

Inciting a riot with the obvious and clear intent to stop the execution of the Twelfth Amendment would definitely meet these criteria. If someone did something like that, of course.

The biggest rebuttal I heard to this argument is that he has not been successfully convicted. Fair enough. "Alleged" criminal then. But does he already meet both definitions of a traitor?

If not being convicted means you didn't do something, then Al Capone was not a gangster. He was convicted of tax evasion. So he and Wesley Snipes (who was also convicted of tax evasion) are basically the same thing? No.[127]

Al Capone was a mobster, but he was never convicted as one. Why? Because RICO didn't come into law until 1970. Probably because of people like Capone.

So, what is RICO? Per a CBS News article, "What is the RICO Act, and how does it impact organized crime?" RICO is the Racketeering Influenced and Corrupt Organizations Act. Originally created to target the Mafia, it ensured leaders of a criminal syndicate could be held accountable for criminal acts under the Act. Thirty-five different crimes could be charged under the RICO Act, to include ones such as robbery, extortion, drug dealing, money laundering, and murder. The act allows prosecutors to charge those who were managing and operating the enterprise with knowledge that the enterprise was engaging in criminal conduct. Even if they were not the ones directly committing the crimes or "getting their hands dirty" in the actual physical criminal act.[128]

So, does this apply to Trump? Well, he has been charged with RICO in the State of Georgia and arrested for it. As of now though, he is considered an innocent man in the eyes of the law (again, for now).[129]

I am going to digress a bit on this one, with one more example. Uday Saddam Hussein was the eldest son of Saddam Hussein.

For many years he was, according to witness allegations, known to kidnap, assault, rape, torture, and murder people.[130]

Was he formally charged and put in prison? Nope. Does this mean he wasn't a rapist and murderer?

Legally, you might argue yes. In any sane definition though, he most certainly was. You don't need a "conviction" to figure this one out. In America, you *do* need a conviction to sentence someone to jail though. And this is a good thing.

"If Trump is a traitor and a criminal, why hasn't he been charged?"

When this was said to me shortly after January 6, he hadn't been. Now he has been arrested, multiple times, for over 90 felonies.

"If trump is a traitor and criminal, why hasn't he been successfully convicted?"

Simple. Could it be that Trump has some of the best lawyers, powerful connections in both the private and public sectors, and is (for now) still a billionaire? Do he and his team have decades of experience skirting accountability for his many "alleged" illegal actions? Do they have an ability to delay, obfuscate, appeal, and otherwise "throw a wrench" in the legal process that is not available to you and me? Did he use his own social media platform and the right-wing media to encourage his millions of MAGA followers to use terrorism against his enemies? And does he use his lawyers to sue, appeal, and otherwise "punish" anyone who dares to speak or act against him?

There you go. "Alleged," just like Uday Hussein.

Here is another example of Trump's innocence, and remorse, over January 6 (this is sarcasm, by the way). His first campaign speech in Waco, Texas, on March 25, 2023, opened with him holding his hand on his heart and reciting the "Pledge of Allegiance" while a recording of the national anthem by the J6 Prison Choir played in the background. The singers were all convicted of charges related to the attack on the Capitol. On a big screen near him, images of the January 6 Capitol attack were then shown. The crowd cheered and chanted USA, USA. The irony is exquisite.

During this speech, Trump protested the "weaponization" of law enforcement, which he said was being used against him and MAGA. He promised that, if reelected, he would serve up vindication for his supporters and punish those who are corrupting our justice system.[131] Pretty sure he may go after more people than just that …

How can anyone not see this as a potentially fascist movement? Isn't he coming right out and saying so?

Sure, he hasn't been convicted of criminal wrongdoing (yet). But was he judged to have been legally responsible of sexual assault and defamation? Yes, per the decision in the *E. Jean Carroll v. Donald J. Trump* civil suit. How did the government, under his thumb, respond to his actions?

In September 2020, government lawyers from the DOJ asserted that Trump had acted in his official capacity while responding to Carroll's accusation. The department said that under the Federal Employees Liability Reform and Tort Compensation Act of 1988 (the "Westfall Act"), it had the right to take the case from Trump's private lawyers and move it to federal court.[132]

Luckily, the judge denied the DOJ's motion.

The way the Westfall Act is supposed to work is this: If a federal employee, acting in good faith and in the scope of their duties, is sued, the federal government can supplant themselves as the defendant. Is sexually assaulting someone, and then defaming them about it on social media, acting in "good faith" or "within the scope of his duties"? What do you think?

If I did that when I was an agent, the government wouldn't have ruled I was acting in the scope of my duties and taken over as the defendant. In fact, I am quite certain they would have fired me.

On July 11, 2023, the DOJ dropped its prior position that Trump had been acting in the scope of his office when making his initial responses to Carroll's allegations.[133]

So, I guess government employees can't get the government to step in for them if they go around making defamatory statements about people's truthful claims.

Trump was also impeached, twice. Both times he was saved by a GOP that clearly ignored all the evidence of his wrongdoings.

The GOP congresspeople who voted to impeach him? They were lambasted on social media and targeted by MAGA. They were voted out of positions and offices by Republicans who are complicit in MAGA terrorism against anyone who goes against them or Donald Trump.

And he has been charged with 91 felony counts. Did I mention that? For some light reading, you can see the status of his many felony charges in the article, "A Guide to the Criminal Cases Against Donald Trump" by PBS.[134]

A little background here from my experiences as a law enforcement officer. A suspect, whom I arrested, was released after the Assistant US Attorney refused to prosecute because of jurisdictional issues. This can also happen just because the prosecutors don't feel the case is a "slam dunk." They base their decision of whether to prosecute on having an overwhelming amount of evidence showing guilt. They are rewarded, as are defense attorneys, for their win record.

They don't want to lose. Neither attorney is looking only for truth and justice. They are fighting a tug of war that only one side can win.

Do you think Trump is a political victim and an upstanding, law-abiding citizen? Or do you think there is an overwhelming amount of evidence showing guilt?

"But what about (fill in the blank with the name of a Democrat or other enemy of MAGA) committing crimes?"

Arrest them too!

The support of a blatant (alleged) career criminal, and (alleged) traitor to his oath and to our Constitution, especially by federal agents and police, has never ceased to amaze me.

As a law enforcement officer, why would they enthusiastically support someone that they should despise?

Because their tribe demands it.

But who leads the tribe?

CHAPTER EIGHTEEN
CULT OF PERSONALITY

IF I COULD SUM UP THIS CHAPTER in one sentence, it would be this:

Please listen to the song "Cult of Personality" by Living Colour.

As a child, I could not understand how people could be convinced to follow a monster like Adolf Hitler or Benito Mussolini. Then, about eighty years after their rule, along comes Donald Trump and MAGA.

I have done my part to fight terrorism. My job involved detecting, deterring, and defeating any criminal or terrorist acts. And gathering intelligence for the same.

When I started at eighteen years old in the army, we were training to fight Russians.

By the 1990s al-Qaeda became a serious problem.[135] Sure, domestic terrorism was a thing, but it was deemed a much smaller problem. And at that time, it was.

IS MAGA A TERRORIST MOVEMENT?

Fast-forward to the first decade of the twenty-first century. My fellow agents and I were, for the most part, "gung-ho" in our mission to find, gather intelligence on, and protect others from known or suspected terrorists (KSTs). This is straight from the DHS website, so it is open source. (I checked, believe me!)

What is a known or suspected terrorist?

"KST" is a term commonly used by law enforcement and intelligence agencies.

First, a "known terrorist" is an individual who has been (a) arrested, charged by information, indicted for, or convicted of a crime related to terrorism and/or terrorist activities by U.S. government or foreign government authorities; or (b) identified as a terrorist or a member of a terrorist organization pursuant to statute, Executive Order, or international legal obligation pursuant to a United Nations Security Council Resolution.

Second, a "suspected terrorist" is an individual who is reasonably suspected to be engaging in, has engaged in, or intends to engage in conduct constituting, in preparation for, in aid of, or related to terrorism and/or terrorist activities.

The use of KST is generally accepted to refer to someone for whom we have a reasonable suspicion to believe that they have or are likely to be engaged in terrorist activity, as that term is defined in US law."[136]

Interesting fact check: Should Donald Trump qualify as a KST at this point? Emphasis on the "known" part of it? Read the KST term above, as defined by DHS (the people who hunt them down) and let me know! Those DHS agents are still hard at work, and I am thankful for them. We were there to defeat terrorists before they could act. Or worst case, as they attacked.

What bothers me is, after Trump became POTUS in 2017, some of these same agents have drawn a blind eye to the rising domestic terror group now known as MAGA.

Every fiber of their being, as it was against al-Qaeda and pseudo-Muslim extremists, should be against this new group as well. In fact, MAGA should be loathed even more—it is a homegrown attack on the very principles of our Constitution and against the wishes of the majority of our population in America. And it is not from foreigners who "hate America," but from Americans who falsely believe they are the biggest patriots.

But, as we discussed, the dual issues of tribalism and pseudo-patriotism put them into a group that believes, and spreads, its own lies.

Now let's add in one more ingredient—the cult of personality.

According to an article in Verywell Mind, "What Is a Cult of Personality?" a cult of personality results from efforts to make a heroic and idealized image of a glorious leader. The leader is unquestioned and receives praise and flattery. Often authoritarian and totalitarian governments are accompanied by these cults of personality. In the past, and present, cults were created using propaganda, patriotism (or what we call pseudo-patriotism), mass media, and government-organized rallies and demonstrations.[137]

So, is MAGA a cult of personality?

Does Trump portray himself as an idealized and heroic leader that demands unquestioning flattery and praise? Has spectacle, propaganda, and patriotism been pushed through the use of mass media? Do the goals and ambitions of an extremist form of pseudo-Christianity get to ride the coattails of MAGA for establishing laws that support their theocracy? Does Trump idolize authoritarian rule, or is he instead a big proponent of fair and free elections and the separation of government powers?

So, what will America become if Trump is reelected in 2024? A failed liberal democracy on its way to becoming something catastrophic. Both for us in America and for other countries abroad. I have said this to MAGA, and they said I was being dramatic. I guess so. People were pretty dramatic about their reactions to losing their freedom to Hitler and Mussolini too.

CHAPTER NINETEEN
LGBTQ+

THE ACRONYM LGBTQ+ is like seeing the "mark of the beast" to most MAGA.[138]

If I make a sign with those letters on it and walk near a MAGA supporter, I bet they will quickly move away or vigorously attack me (verbally and/or physically). Why? Because that is a group they truly despise, and they want them gone. How gone? Preferably holocaust kind of gone.

I have had many discussions with MAGA and of all the people they dislike, LGBTQ+ people seem to be the most reviled. They say it is about the bathroom safety issue, and the transgender swimmers, and about kids seeing LGBTQ+ books, or about kids not being straight, or questioning sexuality at such a young age, and on and on.

So, I asked them at what age it was OK to express "non-straight" characteristics. Or at what age they could act on it, such as their behavior or their medical treatments (hormones, surgeries, etc.).

MAGA made it clear that it wasn't OK at *any* age. So the "small" laws being passed now? Those will lead to the "big" laws in the future. I really do hope 2024 is a good year. If MAGA wins, especially POTUS, you will see exactly what I am talking about in the few short years that follow. You can even show them this book (assuming you can find it, since it will probably be banned or illegal to possess at that point).

But what about getting rid of liberal democracy? To the ignorant this may, at first brush, be taken to mean a democracy of liberals. After all, it has the word "liberal" right in it. Maybe it means a bunch of woke, left-leaning Democrats in charge of the country. As we know at this point, that is not what a liberal democracy means.

Let's take a look at Florida, a clear example of an attempt to destroy liberal democracy as fast as possible. Per the article, "Florida expands 'Don't Say Gay'; House OKs Anti-LGBTQ bills," in AP News, the state has passed several laws that are in line with MAGA and the extreme right, including the "Don't Say Gay" law, which bans classroom instruction about sexual orientation and gender identity in all grades, and a bill on banning people from entering public bathrooms of other than their assigned sex at birth.[139]

Strange and horrifying to see teachers being fired, or under constant fear of being fired, over mentioning anything about these topics. Ostensibly, the reason is the protection of our children and the rights of parents. Sounds reasonable. We don't want our kids learning about mature topics like people not all being straight, or of LGBTQ+ coexisting among them. Or, of Santa not being real. Not yet.[140]

OK. But we also shouldn't be pushing religion down their throats or extolling the evil of not being straight. Those books with LGBTQ+ anything found anywhere in them? Banned, right away! Protect those kids. They see two men holding hands? Hell no.

But a heterosexual couple holding hands? Oh, well *that* is OK. Or a reference to God or the Bible. Totally fine.

How long do you think someone would keep their job as a public teacher, working for a state with these laws, if they brought up those forbidden topics? Or even if they accidentally said something that a child's parent found to be covered under those laws?

If they said something like, "Welcome to the tenth grade. Now I can show you a book with a picture, a reference, something alluding to, or in any way recognizing LGBTQ+. And that they exist and that is OK."

Is that alright to do? Is their job still safe? Or even their freedom? What do you think?

That is the problem. These laws are not just addressing K–3 anymore; they are saying it is verboten in *any* curriculum. Accepting others who aren't like us isn't a weakness, it is what gives America its strength. And those immigrants? Who does MAGA think is going to be paying for their Social Security in old age? The ratio of retirees to workers is already going up as the older generations retire in ever greater numbers each year. Sure, MAGA leaders don't care because MAGA rank and file have made them filthy rich! But, ironically, MAGA "regulars" might want to rethink their immigration stance, especially if they want a "great" American retirement.[141]

Anything from Christianity is OK, like Christmas trees or "Merry Christmas." Anything inclusive of other religions? Like "Happy Holidays," not so much. I used to hear from MAGA every time Christmas rolled around, grousing about the phrase "Happy Holidays."

"They are trying to kill Christmas!"

That utterance is certainly in the top ten of the "stupidest things I have ever heard."

Saying "Merry Christmas" at church? OK, makes sense. Saying it anywhere else, still OK. But maybe, just maybe, the point in saying "Happy Holidays" to complete strangers (who may have any religious affiliation) is to show inclusiveness. A fancy word that really means "having empathy for other people who aren't like you." Is it so hard to say, "Happy Holidays" or "Merry Christmas and Happy Holidays"?

"But our country was founded by Christians!"

There is debate on whether this is true. I mean our money does say, "In God we Trust." And that oath of office? Last sentence: "So help me God."

It's settled then. Our forefathers wanted Christianity to be the established religion of the land! Except for one small, tiny little problem. The very First Amendment in our Constitution that they wrote:

> "Congress shall make no law respecting an establishment of religion, or prohibiting the free exercise thereof; or abridging the freedom of speech, or of the press; or of the right of the people to peaceably assemble, and to petition the Government for a redress of grievances."

Does passing laws allowing a Christmas tree on government property, but saying no to putting up a satanic pentagram count? How about sharing space with Islamic and Jewish holiday ornaments? What about if they just pick and choose, as they do now, what to put up for the religious-based holidays? Should we still be concerned? (We should). Do what you want in the private sector, but the government is supposed to be "neutral" on religion.

Isn't homophobia, passed into law, at its core, the establishment of religion? Let's look at an article from The Gospel Coalition,

"Evangelical and LGBT+ Ally: Why You Can't Be Both." Pseudo-Christianity is clear on homosexuality being a sin. Evangelical Christians embrace some hard-core philosophies from the Old Testament. Yes, according to the Old Testament, the actions of sexual immorality include homosexuality. It also supports the stoning of children who disobeyed their parents. Maybe that's OK in their religion, but modern Americans refer to that as murder.[142]

But now these pseudo-Christians are getting their religious bigotry passed into law. Not being able to even mention or show anything "gay" because of a law? That is unconstitutional.

Thanks to MAGA, now pseudo-religious sin and law can be one and the same. Hello, Theocracy! Doubt me? Just wait a few short years. If they continue their "success," you may see many more of our rights deeply infringed. Especially if you are one of the minority groups they target.

What about peaceful assembly? And the right to petition the government for a redress of grievances? Again, Trump had police clear out protesters, who were peacefully assembled, just for him to have a photo op in front of a church. Holding a Bible, no less.[143]

Too bad he wasn't holding a big copy of the Constitution instead.

Is it OK to hold a Bible? Sure. Would you feel comfortable if the government was doing so *in an official capacity*, standing in front of a church as POTUS? After "moving" peacefully assembled protesters (using tear gas)? How about if you are Muslim, how do you feel? How about if we change all police uniforms to have holy crosses on them and the side of police cars to say: "In God We Trust" or "Thou Shalt Follow My Commandments" instead of some version of "To Serve and Protect"?

This chapter is about LGBTQ+ but, as we have learned, to co-opt MAGA's QAnon motto for a change: "Where we go one, we go all."[144]

IS MAGA A TERRORIST MOVEMENT?

Listen carefully, MAGA: If you are targeting one group of Americans, you are targeting *all* Americans. We will fight back, together, against you!

CHAPTER TWENTY
DEBUNKING MAGA

NOW IT IS TIME TO GO INTO DEBUNKING MAGA "facts" and myths. One of the things MAGA's disciples are taught is that we—anyone who is anti-MAGA or pro-left—are simply "unaware of the truth" and that we are the ones who are deranged and un-American. They call us fascists who want to take away their guns. "Woke" and "Lib-tard." (Lib-tard was my favorite insult. Good one guys, you got me!)

So, let's go into just some of the claims and "truths" that MAGA employs in their arguments for their cause.

We will only go over some of the more common ones I encountered. I can't begin to cover them all. I could, quite literally, write a whole book on just the false and misleading things that MAGA teaches, and their retorts, using verifiable facts. Maybe, if you like my book, I will do that next! A how-to guide, just on debunking MAGA.

1. TDS – Trump Derangement Syndrome

We can jump right into a description of this made-up term using a CNN article, "What is 'Trump Derangement Syndrome' – and do you have it?" Trump Derangement Syndrome is a pejorative term that is used to describe people who have a negative reaction to, or criticism of, Donald Trump. The people that "suffer" from this "syndrome" are perceived to be irrational and to have little regard for Trump's positions, or actions undertaken by him or his former administration.[145] I heard this one. A lot.

This is one of the things, before I learned what the meaning of TDS was, that I had trouble debating with them. This simple accusation is self-fulfilling. If you try having a rational debate with someone in MAGA, or mention a policy or person that is against a MAGA viewpoint, they will claim you have TDS. If you continue to debate, they will be unwilling, or unable, to consider what you calmly say and become adversarial toward you. When you react to their stupidity and aggression by becoming frustrated and angry, voilà! You are deranged. Thus ... TDS.

I wonder if it is in the DSM-5-TR (the standard classification of mental disorders used by mental health professionals)?

So anyway, why is MAGA wrong with their own term? Simple. Because of two false premises.

One, that your negative reaction, or criticism, is irrational. We have read this whole book about just how *rational* our concerns are. Having a viewpoint opposed to MAGA and its objectives is very rational. If you are intelligent.

Two, the presumption that we have little regard toward Trump's actual policy positions, or actions carried out by his administration. What is "regard"? Regard is paying attention to, or considering, something. I would say we are *very* much paying attention and considering his policy positions and actions. In fact, working to stop them is what this book is about.

2. January 6 was a peaceful protest; the media just likes to falsely portray us (MAGA) as terrorists.

As this book has already shown, or as anyone with a TV can attest to, this is clearly not the case.

3. Trump won in 2020, a.k.a. "The Big Lie."[146]

This is a favorite of mine. Logic circles can usually show if someone's thinking makes sense or not. I had this debate with MAGA (more than once). MAGA says that Trump won.

One outcome is that he lost, fair and square (the truth). The other is that he was a victim of a fraudulent election (the lie).

According to the article "AP FACT CHECK: Yes, Trump lost the election despite what he says," he lost the election by 306 to 232 in the Electoral College. This 306 to 232 result was the same margin that Trump beat Clinton with in 2016—an election that he referred to repeatedly as a "landslide" win. His own former attorney general, William Barr, could not find any evidence of widespread election fraud.[147]

So, if it is not the first, then MAGA is right. What would that mean? It would mean that multiple counties (that independently check and verify the votes) in all the states he lost were all able to pull off the biggest fraud *ever*. And do it all under recount after recount, but *only* in the states he lost. If it was such a massive fraud, why weren't *all* the votes recounted, even in states he won? Also, if it really was pulled off, then democracy in America is already dead.

But why didn't the Democrats take the House of Representatives too? I mean, if you have that efficient a fraud scheme, why not take full control of the government?

Doesn't pass the logic test, does it?

CHAPTER TWENTY-ONE
FREEDOM UNDER MAGA RULE

NOW, LET'S TOUCH ON SOME OTHER AREAS where MAGA wants to protect American freedoms. By taking them away.

As an American, we derive our freedoms from the articles and amendments of the Constitution.

First up, again, is Amendment #1: free speech and free press.

An article in *The Diplomat* shows how authoritarian governments around the world manage the spread of information by seizing control of the media (TV and radio stations, social media, mobile phone networks, the internet, etc.). Then they pass laws to solidify this control so that only state-sponsored media is legal.[148]

Why do they do this first? Because once they discredit the media, they can work to shut them down. Then replace them with "state-sponsored" or "state-controlled" media. Who is this state? Well, if Trump is ever POTUS again—MAGA.

The only media that will be allowed, by law, will be extremist-right-supporting "news" agencies.

Once the freedom of the press has been shut down as an *enemy of the people*, they can pass laws (with a Republican majority) to stop these evil, lying, unpatriotic, non-MAGA-supporting, news organizations from spreading "fake news." Maybe put them in jail for it even.

If POTUS says, for example, the press is "the enemy of the people," as Trump tweeted in 2017 and again as POTUS in 2019, is that not an attack on the First Amendment?[149] I have asked MAGA this very question. Their answer is "No, it is not." OK, so then I ask the opposite: "How is POTUS saying that *not* an attack on the First Amendment"? They, understandably, could not answer. Because the answer is in the question. If a person in position of power (POTUS definitely qualifies) makes clear the government's position is one of the free press being the enemy, that does qualify as an attack on the First Amendment.

"He never said that." I had one MAGA say that to me.

I couldn't pull up the quote at the time, so he accused me of making false statements and having Trump Derangement Syndrome.

This is why I wrote this book, so you can have answers to their "Owning the Libs" nonsense, in addition to defeating MAGA.

Here is Donald Trump's quote, captured by the very same media he and MAGA despise:

> "The press is doing everything within their power to fight the magnificence of the phrase, MAKE AMERICA GREAT AGAIN! They can't stand the fact that this Administration has done more than virtually any other Administration in its first 2yrs. They are truly the ENEMY OF THE PEOPLE!"
>
> — Donald J. Trump (@realDonaldTrump) April 5, 2019[150]

This was on April 5, 2019. As president of the United States. Why were he and his MAGA followers so angry at the press? I mean, if the press said something that wasn't true, shouldn't they have successfully sued them for slander or libel?

The reason they are so angry is that it is the job, and First Amendment right, of the free press to report on news stories.

When they produce an article that makes MAGA look bad because of things they actually said or did, they are just holding them accountable. Just like I am using my first amendment right to publish this book and say the things I am saying to hold them accountable.

So, what does MAGA do? Well, use a defamatory label for them of course!

The "Lamestream Media."

As opposed to the right-wing media, which never lies to anyone and always tells the "real truth."

MAGA doesn't like being held accountable. When the free press records things they say and do, it makes it difficult for them to lie about what they said, or did, later. I mean, I just brought up a quote from the media from over four years ago, showing Trump's own tweet. No matter how many times MAGA repeats a lie, it does not make it true. They also don't like people looking too deeply into any possible criminal behavior.

But no worries. MAGA has a plan. The first step is discrediting their enemies. The steps after that will be to control the government, and then to pass laws to eliminate those enemies.

Another example of MAGA attacking our freedoms relates to a court case from 1958, *Kent v. Dulles*, which concluded that "the right to travel is a part of the 'liberty' of which the citizen cannot be deprived without due process of law under the Fifth Amendment."[151]

So, why do I bring this up? MAGA say they are all about freedom. So why are states passing laws about charging people for leaving the states to have an abortion? Don't worry, I am not going into a pro-life versus pro-choice debate here. I am talking about the right to leave your state for any reason you want. Any time you want. And that, in and of itself, is not a crime.

In Colorado marijuana is legal. In Kansas, the state next to it, it is illegal. If you go from Kansas to Colorado to use marijuana, it is exactly the same as if you travel from Texas to Colorado for an abortion. You are going from one state where something is illegal, to another where it is legal.[152] [153]

So, if they can charge someone for doing something legal in a different state because the citizen used their "right to travel" to leave the state where it wasn't permitted, isn't that person's freedom of movement being infringed upon?

The laws being passed by (Republican-controlled) state legislatures that allow for prosecution for leaving the state to commit an act that is legal in the state they are traveling to (but not the one they reside in) is definitely violating this. Our Constitution applies to all fifty states, whether they like it or not.

MAGA wants to crush your constitutional rights. Not my opinion, it is a fact. This chapter illustrates this. Are you a MAGA member and don't like me saying this? Then stop doing it.

CHAPTER TWENTY-TWO
END GAME

I PROMISED YOU AT THE BEGINNING of our book that I would tell you how to fight MAGA terrorism. Now I shall.

Before I explain this in detail, I want to make one thing very clear: I am *not* advocating for the illegal use of violence or force, terrorism of any kind, or committing any crime! The whole point of our fight is to support the laws of the land that already exist, and to prevent unjust laws from being passed. Legally, by voting and by peacefully speaking up.

So, here are the steps to fight MAGA, the domestic terrorist organization that it is:

1. Identification
2. Methodology
3. Vulnerabilities
4. Isolation
5. Destruction

1. Identification

Who are its members? In what country are they primarily based? Do other states or countries give them support? What are their stated objectives? Do they use terrorism to win and implement those objectives?

MAGA members are mostly Americans with a conservative political viewpoint, even reactionary. They are based in the US. Other countries hostile to western civilization also support them. Russia, per the FBI, was, and is, heavily involved in misinformation and cyberattacks to aid the MAGA movement.[154]

We defined MAGA's intent already in the first chapter, but in summary, it is a reactionary, far-right movement to return us to the way America used to be in "the good old days."

Do they use terrorism to win and implement those objectives? Yes, we have exhaustively covered how they meet the definition and intent of terrorism.

2. Methodology

What means are they using to affect these changes? Beyond just establishing that they use terrorism, how many operators are there and what weapons do they use? How are they funded and are others providing aid and comfort to them? What kind and how much? Do they have strong support in their own country (internal) and/or support from foreign countries (external)?

The exact number of MAGA is hard to nail down. The closest I could come was based on an article in *The Washington Post* by Phillip Bump, "Figuring out how many 'MAGA' Republicans there actually are." Here are his estimations:

About 19 percent of US adults are Republican, a party clearly controlled by or partial to MAGA. An additional 26 percent are Republican-leaning Independents, bringing the total Republican support to 45 percent. About 7 percent of American adults somewhat or strongly approved of the MAGA January 6 terror attack, while the number of active terrorists was estimated to be somewhere in the thousands. The Republican Party provides funding, aid, support, and/or comfort directly, or indirectly, to MAGA. So they have strong internal support.[155]

We know Russia is providing external support. But any country with a vested interest in destroying or limiting America's involvement in foreign or sovereign democracy could conceivably also provide "aid" through misinformation or other means.

We have covered how MAGA's weapons are primarily social media and control of governments, but they have used physical weapons for terror as well. We have seen them use everything from police riot shields, to barricades, or other weapons. Some carried batons or firearms. One carried a hammer into a senator's home.

They have used vehicles to surround and stop a bus. Many MAGA I have talked to have already said they are OK with civil war if Trump doesn't take back the White House. And since they are huge supporters of unrestricted access to all guns, via the Second Amendment, many MAGA have access to firearms.

3.Vulnerabilities

Not only what are their vulnerabilities as a terrorist organization, but what are our vulnerabilities as their target?

Can we "harden" a target to make it more difficult to strike or to mitigate the amount of damage? In what areas are they vulnerable?

Where can we attack them to lessen, or stop, their ability to fight or harm us?

What are our vulnerabilities?
Our vulnerabilities are many. We are vulnerable to them terrorizing voters and our democratic institutions (such as the Capitol) and using their aggressive tactics—tactics encouraging both our nonparticipation in government and silence on issues important to MAGA. They probably won't take kindly to this book, or its author, for example.

We are vulnerable to their attempts to seize voting machines, not count our votes, or just to bypass the vote entirely and use fake electors. How can we prove this allegation? Well, with the conviction of the prosecution's new star witness, Sidney Powell. She was an attorney for Trump and has pleaded guilty to multiple charges in the Georgia election subversion case. This is covered in detail in the CNN article, "Trump attorney Sidney Powell pleads guilty in Georgia election subversion case."[156]

They have also tried to limit access to voting in areas known to be non-Republican, using such methods as opposing mail-in voting or trying to gut the Voting Rights Act, which outlawed the discriminatory voting practices adopted in many southern states after the Civil War.[157]

What are their vulnerabilities?
The biggest is a free and fair liberal democracy and, for now, a majority of voters who recognize the threat to it and vote accordingly. We also need to continue the excellent work of ensuring the validity of, and full access to, fair voting. The other is the law. Not only is

terrorism wrong, but it is also illegal. Turn them in (call the police) when you are aware of their illegal behavior.

Their views can easily be debunked through facts and their methods are predictable. The lies and untrue "facts" they receive (mostly from right-wing media outlets), and their beliefs are easily disproven by those not in the movement. Their premise is based on lies and can be invalidated publicly. We can "harden" our position through knowledge about MAGA and by banding together to negate their actions. We can, and must, vote.

4. Isolation

Before we can attack, we must isolate the enemy. We need to know who they are, and where they are. We must pinpoint this before we can attack or counterattack. And we also must eliminate, or minimize, collateral damage (damage to people and things that are not our target).

We have identified who MAGA is and who supports them. Now we must isolate them to act without harming "innocents," or those that are not MAGA/MAGA supporters. We are not in a hot war (violent, open warfare), yet. So, in this case, isolation simply means making sure our actions are aimed at them and not destructive to the greater whole (collateral damage). In this case I am referring to thousands of active terrorists, such as those involved in the January 6 attack, that DHS and the FBI are already investigating and prosecuting. And to the millions of MAGA members who support the illegal and unconstitutional actions of their members, such as the actions that occurred on January 6.

To a much lesser extent, we must include those who directly and indirectly support MAGA by funding them or voting Republican, as long as voting Republican is a vote for Trump and MAGA.

5. Destruction

Can we apprehend, seize, or destroy the enemy's members, weapons, equipment, transportation, support, logistical systems, and funding? Can we assist others who also fight them?

Apprehend, seize, or destroy. The job and mandate to investigate, apprehend, seize, or destroy, is entrusted in the agents of government. An agent is a person acting or doing business for another. We give the authority to investigate and apprehend (including using force, as needed) to our government. We give power to the courts and to law enforcement and the military. We hold them accountable to go after the law-breaking members of MAGA. As for most of us, who are regular civilians and not law enforcement, we can "turn them in" whenever they commit illegal acts, with whatever evidence you have (to include your testimony in court, if need be).

What about when MAGA surrounds a "Biden bus," or when they terrorize citizens? Again, if you can safely document it, do. And call 911. Leave the phone on, you are being recorded and so are they. The officers that show up? Yup, in most jurisdictions now, they are filming too with their body cameras. What if the police are not doing anything? That is nonfeasance. Film them and the bad guys (from a safe distance). Report it higher in their chain of command and be willing to post it to social media. But please show the entirety of what you saw, all the details matter.

Most of this fight against MAGA, by average Americans, will be waged by resisting and reporting MAGA acts of terrorism and by voting in *every* election you are authorized to. In short, I am sorry to have to say this, but you should vote against the Republican Party. They are now the Party of Trump and MAGA. In a two-party system like the one America has now, it means voting Democrat to stop them. Hopefully, for Republicans' sake, they will get their party back one day from the clutches of MAGA. I read an article with a good point. Even if you like a particular Republican candidate, you must vote against their party if that party supports the terrorism, or the illegal actions, of MAGA.

Am I telling you how to vote?!

No. But I *am* giving you the information to make you aware of what that vote will support. It is up to us to stop them. No one can tell you how you must vote, but your vote is one of the most powerful tools in our democracy! Use it wisely.

Together, we stopped MAGA from taking over America in 2020. Take a hard look at what the Republican Party supports, and what they did during the impeachments of Donald Trump—how they wrongly defended him, twice. Look at the laws and the people they support. Look at how they are chipping away at your freedoms, piece by precious piece. Look at how they have pushed to pass the laws they want, and to get rid of laws they don't.

Look at all the ways Trump, when he was POTUS, tried to either weaken, disable, or control the different branches of government to ensure more power in the presidency and in his party. Look at the Republican Party that enabled, and *still* enables, him.

If you want to destroy MAGA, call them out.

But more importantly—vote them out. Every chance you get.

Now when MAGA asks for your sources in an argument (few truly debate), I hope you turn to this book. I also hope it can save you from those debates completely. Just tell them to read this book. If they are still upset with you, have them reach out to me instead. I will be happy to chat.

I also want to share an epiphany that I had. A lot of my angst was from working with agents who supported MAGA. Why did it affect me? Because I let it affect me. Put MAGA in the same mental category as any other terrorist group. Do you care what al-Qaeda or Hamas think of you? Didn't think so. Don't care what MAGA thinks of you either. Approaching it this way will save you from their "Owning the Libs" arguments. If you don't listen to fatwa-supporting-pseudo-Muslim extremists when they preach Sharia law, then don't listen to MAGA when they tout MAGA as the "one true way" either. We know better.

    Thank you for reading my book. I hope it is a useful guide. Together, we can put an end to MAGA's reign of terror and bring law, peace, acceptance, and freedom for all back to our great nation.

NOTES

1. George Washington's Mount Vernon, "Quotes," accessed January 17, 2024, https://www.mountvernon.org/library/digitalhistory/past-projects/quotes/article/there-is-nothing-so-likely-to-produce-peace-as-to-be-well-prepared-to-meet-an-enemy/.

2. David Bauder, Randall Chase, and Geoff Mulvihill, "Fox, Dominion reach $787M settlement over election claims," AP, April 18, 2023, https://apnews.com/article/fox-news-dominion-lawsuit-trial-trump-2020-0ac71f75acfacc52ea80b3e747fb0afe.

3. Glenn Kessler, Salvador Rizzo, and Meg Kelly, "Trump's false or misleading claims total 30,573 over 4 years," *The Washington Post*, January 24, 2021, https://www.washingtonpost.com/politics/2021/01/24/trumps-false-or-misleading-claims-total-30573-over-four-years/.

4   Marmaduke William Pickthall, translator. *The Qur'an*, MobileReference, 2010.

5   André Munro, "liberal democracy." In *Encyclopaedia Britannica Online*, History & Society, last updated October 13, 2023, https://www.britannica.com/topic/liberal-democracy.

6   Bible Gateway, Hebrews 11:1, King James Version, accessed February 14, 2024, https://www.biblegateway.com/passage/?search=Hebrews+11%3A1&version=KJV.

7   Donald L. Fixico, "When Native Americans Were Slaughtered in the Name of 'Civilization,'" History.com, July 11, 2023, https://www.history.com/news/native-americans-genocide-united-states.

8   *Encyclopedia of Alabama*, Civil Rights, "Segregation (Jim Crow)," accessed February 14, 2024, https://encyclopediaofalabama.org/article/segregation-jim-crow/.

9   *Encyclopaedia Britannica Online*, History & Society, "al-Qaeda," last updated January 13, 2024, https://www.britannica.com/topic/al-Qaeda.

10 Adam Volle, "MAGA movement." In *Encyclopaedia Britannica Online*, History & Society, last updated January 16, 2024, https://www.britannica.com/topic/MAGA-movement.

11 Paul D. Miller, "What Is Christian Nationalism?" *Christianity Today*, February 3, 2021, https://www.christianitytoday.com/ct/2021/february-web-only/what-is-christian-nationalism.html.

NOTES

12 U.S. Senate Staff Report, *Examining the U.S. Capitol Attack, A Review of the Security, Planning, and Response Failures on January 6,* accessed January 17, 2024, https://www.hsgac.senate.gov/wp-content/uploads/imo/media/doc/HSGAC&RulesFullReport_ExaminingU.S.CapitolAttack.pdf.

13 *Merriam-Webster.com Dictionary*, s.v. "woke (*a.*)," "terrorism (*n.*)," "counterterrorism (*n.*)," accessed January 17, 2024, https://www.merriam-webster.com/dictionary/woke, https://www.merriam-webster.com/dictionary/terrorism, https://www.merriam-webster.com/dictionary/counterterrorism.

14 Jessica Taylor, "Trump Calls for 'Total and Complete Shutdown of Muslims Entering' U.S.," NPR, December 7, 2015, https://www.npr.org/2015/12/07/458836388/trump-calls-for-total-and-complete-shutdown-of-muslims-entering-u-s.

15 Adam Volle, "MAGA movement." In *Encyclopaedia Britannica Online*, History & Society, last updated January 16, 2024, https://www.britannica.com/topic/MAGA-movement.

16 Dictionary.com, s.v. "pseudo (*a.*)," "patriotism (*n.*)," accessed January 17, 2024, https://www.dictionary.com/browse/pseudo, https://www.dictionary.com/browse/patriotism.

17 Dictionary.com, s.v. "co-opt (*v.*)," accessed January 17, 2024, https://www.dictionary.com/browse/co-opt.

18 U.S. Department of Veterans Affairs, *Guidelines for Display of the Flag*, Washington, D.C., Public Law 94-344, Federal Flag Code, https://www.va.gov/opa/publications/celebrate/flagdisplay.pdf.

19 Avi Shafran, "Some Trump supporters are co-opting the American flag. Nazis once did that, too," NBC News, June 14, 2021, https://www.nbcnews.com/think/opinion/some-trump-supporters-are-co-opting-american-flag-nazis-once-ncna1270741.

20 Kyle Sallee, "Decoding Hate: Understanding the Far-Right Symbology of January 6," American University, Washington, D.C., July 1, 2021, https://www.american.edu/sis/centers/security-technology/decoding-hate-understanding-far-right-symbology.cfm.

21 Wynne Davis and Scott Simon, "Here's what 'Let's Go, Brandon' actually means and how it made its way to Congress," NPR, October 31, 2021, https://www.npr.org/2021/10/30/1050782613/why-the-lets-go-brandon-chant-turned-meme-can-be-heard-on-the-floor-of-congress.

22 Olga R. Rodriguez, "Man who attacked Pelosi's husband is convicted of federal assault and attempted kidnapping charges," AP, November 16, 2023, U.S. News, https://apnews.com/article/pelosi-depape-hammer-attack-verdict-3e9cba213130b6db90197d17b09640fa.

NOTES

23 Gillian Flaccus, "Portland's Grim Reality: 100 Days of Protests, Many Violent," AP, September 4, 2020, https://apnews.com/article/virus-outbreak-ap-top-news-race-and-ethnicity-id-state-wire-or-state-wire-b57315d97dd2146c4a89b4636faa7b70.

24 U.S. Department of Justice, "Department of Justice Closes Investigation into the Death of Ashli Babbitt," DOJ, United States Attorney's Office, D.C., April 14, 2021, https://www.justice.gov/usao-dc/pr/department-justice-closes-investigation-death-ashli-babbitt.

25 Chris Cillizza and Brenna Williams, "15 times Donald Trump praised authoritarian rulers," CNN, July 2, 2019, https://www.cnn.com/2019/07/02/politics/donald-trump-dictators-kim-jong-un-vladimir-putin/index.html.

26 Kevin Breuninger, "Trump chief of staff said the president thought Pence 'deserves' chants of 'hang Mike Pence' on Jan. 6, ex-aide testifies," CNBC, June 28, 2022, https://www.cnbc.com//2022/06/28/jan-6-hearing-trump-thought-pence-deserved-chants-to-hang-him-aide-says.html.

27 Rogé Karma, "Why America Abandoned the Greatest Economy in History," *The Atlantic*, November 25, 2023, https://www.theatlantic.com/ideas/archive/2023/11/new-deal-us-economy-american-dream/676051/.

28 Elizabeth Grace Matthew, "I'm a conservative Catholic mom. 'Trad wives' promote unrealistic stereotypes." *USA Today*, July 19, 2023, https://www.usatoday.com/story/opinion/voices/2023/07/19/trad-wife-tiktok-promotes-unrealistic-vision-marriage-family/70419993007/.

29 Cullen Peele, "Roundup of Anti-LGBTQ+ Legislation Advancing in States Across the Country," Human Rights Campaign, May 23, 2023, https://www.hrc.org/press-releases/roundup-of-anti-lgbtq-legislation-advancing-in-states-across-the-country.

30 Center for American Progress, "Maga Extremism in Schools: Republican-Led States Are Banning Books, Not Guns," CAP Action 20, September 7, 2022, https://www.americanprogressaction.org/article/maga-extremism-in-schools-republican-led-states-are-banning-books-not-guns/.

31 Ray Bradbury, *Fahrenheit 451* (New York: Simon & Schuster, 2012).

32 Danyelle Solomon, Connor Maxwell, and Abril Castro, "Systemic Inequality: Displacement, Exclusion, and Segregation. How America's Housing System Undermines Wealth Building in Communities of Color," Center for American Progress, August 7, 2019, https://www.americanprogress.org/article/systemic-inequality-displacement-exclusion-segregation/.

NOTES

33 Rakesh Kochhar and Stella Sechopoulos, "How the American middle class has changed in the past five decades," Pew Research Center, April 20, 2022, https://www.pewresearch.org/short-reads/2022/04/20/how-the-american-middle-class-has-changed-in-the-past-five-decades/.

34 Encyclopaedia Britannica, "The Emancipation Proclamation," Wars, Battles & Armed Conflicts, accessed February 14, 2024, https://www.britannica.com/event/American-Civil-War/The-Emancipation-Proclamation.

35 Abraham Lincoln Online, "Last Public Address," Speeches & Writings, Washington, D.C., accessed February 14, 2024, https://www.abrahamlincolnonline.org/lincoln/speeches/last.htm#:~:text=No%20one%20man%20has%20authority,manner%2C%20and%20means%20of%20reconstruction.

36 National Geographic Society, "The Ku Klux Klan," *National Geographic*, last updated October 19, 2023, https://education.nationalgeographic.org/resource/ku-klux-klan/.

37 History.com Editors, "Segregation in the United States," History.com, last updated January 12, 2023, https://www.history.com/topics/black-history/segregation-united-states.

38 Plessy v. Ferguson, 163 U.S. 537 (1896), National Archives, last reviewed February 8, 2022, https://www.archives.gov/milestone-documents/plessy-v-ferguson.

39 Brown v. Board of Education, 347 U.S. 483 (1954), National Archives, last reviewed November 22, 2021, https://www.archives.gov/milestone-documents/brown-v-board-of-education.

40 History.com Editors, "Black History Milestones: Timeline," History.com, last updated January 24, 2024, https://www.history.com/topics/black-history/black-history-milestones.

41 Clarence Lusane, "It's No Mystery Why Racists Have Fallen In Love With Trump's Republican Party," *The Nation*, October 11, 2023, https://www.thenation.com/article/politics/racist-republicans-donald-trump/.

42 Lindsay Kornick, "WaPo article claims 'Make America Great Again' means return to 1950s when things were 'great only for some,'" Fox News, Donald Trump, July 26, 2022, https://www.foxnews.com/media/wapo-article-claims-make-america-great-again-means-return-1950s-when-things-great-only-some.

43 Derald Wing Sue, "Trump, MAGA and the insidious underbelly of white supremacy in America," *The Hill*, November 28, 2023, https://thehill.com/opinion/campaign/4330735-trump-maga-and-the-insidious-underbelly-of-white-supremacy-in-america/.

NOTES

44 The White House, "Remarks by President Biden Honoring the Legacy of Senator John McCain and the Work We Must Do Together to Strengthen Our Democracy," The White House, September 28, 2023, https://www.whitehouse.gov/briefing-room/speeches-remarks/2023/09/28/remarks-by-president-biden-honoring-the-legacy-of-senator-john-mccain-and-the-work-we-must-do-together-to-strengthen-our-democracy/.

45 Jeff Neal, "'I do solemnly swear'—The oath of office and what it means," Federal News Network, January 4, 2021, https://federalnewsnetwork.com/commentary/2021/01/i-do-solemnly-swear-the-oath-of-office-and-what-it-means/.

46 *Appointment Affidavits*, U.S. Office of Personnel Management, Standard Form 61, revised August 2002, https://www.opm.gov/forms/pdf_fill/sf61.pdf.

47 National Constitution Center, Article VI, Debts, Supremacy, Oaths, Religious Tests, accessed January 17, 2024, https://constitutioncenter.org/the-constitution/articles/article-vi.

48 National Constitution Center, Fourteenth Amendment, Section 3, Citizenship Rights, Equal Protection, Apportionment, Civil War Debt, accessed January 17, 2024, https://constitutioncenter.org/the-constitution/amendments/amendment-xiv#amendment-section-3.

49 Max Elbaum, "MAGA Authoritarian Rule or Third Reconstruction?" *Convergence*, June 20, 2023, https://convergencemag.com/articles/maga-authoritarian-rule-or-third-reconstruction/.

50 Third Way, "2020 Thematic Brief: Trump Investigations," Third Way, The National Security Program, September 17, 2020, https://www.thirdway.org/primer/2020-thematic-brief-trump-investigations.

51 The Associated Press, "Capitol rioter plans 2024 run as a Libertarian candidate in Arizona's 8th congressional district," AP, last updated November 12, 2023, https://apnews.com/article/capitol-rioter-arizona-congress-chansley-33de9a9f4ff1ea35cd12d9719a2f2987.

52 *Merriam-Webster*, s.v. "libertarian (*n*.)," accessed January 17, 2024, https://www.merriam-webster.com/dictionary/libertarian.

53 Lauren Irwin, "Judge rules Trump can stay on Michigan ballot, rejects insurrection clause challenge," The Hill, State Watch, November 14, 2023, https://thehill.com/homenews/state-watch/4310114-judge-rules-trump-stay-michigan-ballot/.

54 Steve Karnowski and Nicholas Riccardi, "Minnesota Supreme Court dismisses 'insurrection clause' challenge and allows Trump on 2024 ballot," *PBS New Hour*, November 8, 2023, https://www.pbs.org/newshour/politics/minnesota-supreme-court-dismisses-insurrection-clause-challenge-and-allows-trump-on-2024-ballot.

NOTES

55 Josh Gerstein and Alexander Ward, "Supreme Court has voted to overturn abortion rights, draft opinion shows," *Politico*, last updated May 3, 2022, https://www.politico.com/news/2022/05/02/supreme-court-abortion-draft-opinion-00029473.

56 Alex Swoyer, "Judge keeps Trump on Colorado primary ballot, says insurrection clause doesn't apply to presidency," *The Washington Times*, Election, November 17, 2023, https://www.washingtontimes.com/news/2023/nov/17/sarah-b-wallace-colorado-judge-rejects-insurrectio/.

57 Caitlin Yilek, "What to know about the Colorado Supreme Court's Trump ruling, and what happens next," CBS News, last updated December 20, 2023, https://www.cbsnews.com/news/trump-colorado-supreme-court-ruling-what-happens-next/.

58 Carrie Johnson, "Supreme Court justices appear skeptical of effort to remove Trump from a state ballot," NPR, February 8, 2024, https://www.npr.org/2024/02/08/1229176555/supreme-court-trump-colorado-ballot.

59 Margaret Atwood, *The Handmaid's Tale* (New York: Anchor Books, a division of Penguin Random House LLC, 1998).

60 Steven Simon and Jonathan Stevenson, "The Threat of Civil Breakdown Is Real," *Politico*, April 21, 2023, https://www.politico.com/news/magazine/2023/04/21/political-violence-2024-magazine-00093028.

61 Dictionary.com, s.v. "terrorism (*n.*)," accessed January 17, 2024, https://www.dictionary.com/browse/terrorism.

62 U.S. Department of Justice, "Three Years Since the Jan. 6 Attack on the Capitol," DOJ, last updated January 5, 2024, https://www.justice.gov/usao-dc/36-months-jan-6-attack-capitol-0.

63 Linda So, "Trump-inspired death threats are terrorizing election workers," Reuters, June 11, 2021, https://www.reuters.com/investigates/special-report/usa-trump-georgia-threats/.

64 Acacia Coronado, "Texas city settles lawsuit over police response to Trump supporters surrounding Biden bus in 2020," AP, October 18, 2023, https://apnews.com/article/election-2020-biden-trump-political-intimidation-lawsuit-7a705ba3b8f9be2fe3c726c897a15fe5.

65 Dictionary.com, s.v. "tribalism (n.)," accessed January 17, 2024, https://www.dictionary.com/browse/tribalism.

66 Meg Anderson and Nick McMillan, "1,000 people have been charged for the Capitol riot. Here's where their cases stand," NPR, Investigations, March 25, 2023, https://www.npr.org/2023/03/25/1165022885/1000-defendants-january-6-capitol-riot.

67 Quentin Young, "MAGA cops are a mega threat," Colorado Newsline, September 29, 2022, https://coloradonewsline.com/2022/09/29/maga-cops-are-a-mega-threat/.

NOTES

68 Kabir Khanna, Anthony Salvanto, Jennifer De Pinto, and Fred Backus, "Trump maintains dominant lead among 2024 Republican candidates as GOP field narrows: CBS News poll," CBS News, November 6, 2023, https://www.cbsnews.com/news/poll-trump-leads-republican-field-gop-2023-11-06/.

69 Hannah Getahun, "Trump had access to national security information not seen by most American citizens. Here are the different levels of security clearances and who is allowed to have them." Business Insider, August 12, 2022, https://www.businessinsider.com/what-are-security-clearances-and-who-is-allowed-to-have-them-2022-8#.

70 Kathryn Watson, "Can Trump still become president if he's convicted of a crime or found liable in a civil case?" CBS News, last updated June 13, 2023, https://www.cbsnews.com/news/can-trump-still-run-for-president-if-convicted-felony-2024/.

71 National Archives, "Global War on Terror," accessed January 17, 2024, https://www.georgewbushlibrary.gov/research/topic-guides/global-war-terror.

72 The American Presidency Project, "Special Message to the Congress on Crime and Law Enforcement." APP, accessed January 17, 2024, https://www.presidency.ucsb.edu/documents/special-message-the-congress-crime-and-law-enforcement.

73 Juhohn Lee, "America has spent over a trillion dollars fighting the war on drugs. 50 years later, drug use in the U.S. is climbing again." CNBC, last updated June 17, 2021, https://www.cnbc.com/2021/06/17/the-us-has-spent-over-a-trillion-dollars-fighting-war-on-drugs.html.

74 Library of Congress, "National Policy Institute (NPI)/AltRight.com," Library of Congress, Washington, D.C., summary retrieved on October 7, 2019, https://www.loc.gov/item/lcwaN0018510/.

75 Drew Millard, "We Asked a White Supremacist What He Thinks of Donald Trump," *Vice Digital*, December 10, 2015, https://www.vice.com/en/article/bnp33d/we-asked-a-white-supremacist-what-he-thought-of-donald-trump-1210.

76 Eliza Collins, "David Duke: Voting against Trump is 'treason to your heritage,'" *Politico*, February 25, 2016, https://www.politico.com/story/2016/02/david-duke-trump-219777.

77 Andy Sullivan and Jason Lange, "Trump holds wide lead in race for Republican nomination: Reuters/Ipsos poll," Reuters, January 10, 2024, https://www.reuters.com/world/us/trump-holds-wide-lead-race-republican-nomination-reutersipsos-2024-01-10/.

78 Naval History and Heritage Command, "The Gulf War 1990-1991 (Operation Desert Shield/Desert Storm)," NHHC, accessed January 17, 2024, https://www.history.navy.mil/our-collections/art/exhibits/conflicts-and-operations/the-gulf-war-1990-1991--operation-desert-shield--desert-storm-.html.

NOTES

79 CIA, "Terrorist Organizations," CIA.gov, The World Factbook, References, accessed January 17, 2024, https://www.cia.gov/the-world-factbook/references/terrorist-organizations/.

80 "Domestic Violent Extremism," U.S. Department of the Treasury, Terrorism and Illicit Finance, accessed January 17, 2024, https://home.treasury.gov/policy-issues/terrorism-and-illicit-finance/domestic-violent-extremism.

81 Mike Levine, "'No Blame?' ABC News finds 54 cases invoking 'Trump' in connection with violence, threats, alleged assaults." ABC News, May 30, 2020, https://abcnews.go.com/Politics/blame-abc-news-finds-17-cases-invoking-trump/story?id=58912889.

82 By Melissa Quinn and Graham Kates, "Trump's 4 indictments in detail: A quick-look guide to charges, trial dates and key players for each case," CBS News, September 5, 2023, https://www.cbsnews.com/news/trump-indictments-details-guide-charges-trial-dates-people-case/.

83 Tom Norton, "Fact Check: Do Security Clearances Allow Trump to Keep Files at Mar-a-Lago?" *Newsweek*, October 13, 2022, https://www.newsweek.com/fact-check-do-security-clearances-allow-trump-keep-files-mar-lago-1751602.

84 CIA, "Terrorist Organizations," CIA.gov, The World Fact Book (2022 Archive), References, access January 17, 2024, https://www.cia.gov/the-world-factbook/about/archives/2022/references/terrorist-organizations/.

85 Josh Gerstein, "Why DOJ is avoiding domestic terrorism sentences for Jan. 6 defendants," *Politico*, January 4, 2022, https://www.politico.com/news/2022/01/04/doj-domestic-terrorism-sentences-jan-6-526407.

86 Jacob Ware and Ania Zolyniak, "Jan. 6 and Beyond: Why the U.S. Should Pass Domestic Terrorism Legislation," Lawfare, May 28, 2023, https://www.lawfaremedia.org/article/jan.-6-and-beyond-why-the-u.s.-should-pass-domestic-terrorism-legislation.

87 *Merriam-Webster.com*, s.v. "nonfeasance (*n.*)," accessed January 17, 2024, https://www.merriam-webster.com/dictionary/nonfeasance.

88 U.S. Department of Justice, "A Sitting President's Amenability to Indictment and Criminal Prosecution," DOJ, Office of Legal Counsel, October 16, 2000, https://www.justice.gov/olc/opinion/sitting-president%E2%80%99s-amenability-indictment-and-criminal-prosecution.

89 HRC Staff, "The Real List of Trump's 'Unprecedented Steps' for the LGBTQ Community, Human Rights Campaign, June 11, 2020, https://www.hrc.org/news/the-list-of-trumps-unprecedented-steps-for-the-lgbtq-community.

90 Myrna Pérez, "7 Years of Gutting Voting Rights," Brennan Center for Justice, June 25, 2020, https://www.brennancenter.org/our-work/analysis-opinion/7-years-gutting-voting-rights.

NOTES

91 Mary Clare Jalonick and Lisa Mascaro, "GOP blocks Capitol riot probe, displaying loyalty to Trump," AP, May 28, 2021, https://apnews.com/article/michael-pence-donald-trump-capitol-siege-government-and-politics-4798a8617bacf27bbb576a4b805b85d9.

92 Clare Foran and Ted Barrett, "Senate Republicans block domestic terrorism prevention bill in key vote," CNN, last updated May 26, 2022, https://www.cnn.com/2022/05/26/politics/senate-domestic-terrorism-bill-vote/index.html.

93 Geoffrey Skelley, "With Cheney's Loss, Just 2 House Republicans Who Voted To Impeach Trump Are On the Ballot In November," FiveThirtyEight, August 16, 2022, https://fivethirtyeight.com/features/with-cheneys-loss-just-2-house-republicans-who-voted-to-impeach-trump-are-on-the-ballot-in-november/.

94 Steve Vladeck, "Trump and Republicans' Electoral College election objections betray conservative legal thought," NBC News, last updated January 7, 2021, https://www.nbcnews.com/think/opinion/trump-senate-gop-s-electoral-college-vote-objections-betray-conservative-ncna1252927.

95 Jarret Bencks, "The Proud Boys, the Oath Keepers and jihadist extremists: What they have in common and what they don't," *BrandeisNOW*, June 13, 2022, http://www.brandeis.edu/how/2022/June/klausen-proud-boys-oath-keepers-jihdists.html.

96 Glenn C. Altschuler, "Republicans are weaponization wannabes, *The Hill*, July 2, 2023, https://thehill.com/opinion/criminal-justice/4076603-republicans-are-weaponization-wannabes/.

97 Ingrid Jacques, "Liz Cheney: GOP must move beyond Trump's 'cult of personality,'" *USA Today*, June 5, 2023, https://www.usatoday.com/story/opinion/2023/06/05/cheney-says-gop-needs-sanity-not-trump/70277960007/.

98 Dictionary.com, s.v. "coup d' état (*n.*)," "self-coup (*n.*)," accessed January 17, 2024, https://www.dictionary.com/browse/coup-d-etat, https://www.dictionary.com/browse/self-coup.

99 Sophie Lewis, "Joe Biden breaks Obama's record for most votes ever cast for a U.S. presidential candidate," CBS News, last updated December 7, 2020, https://www.cbsnews.com/news/joe-biden-popular-vote-record-barack-obama-us-presidential-election-donald-trump/.

100 Melissa Quinn, Kathryn Watson, Nikole Killion, Caitlin Yilek, and Caroline Linton, "Mike Johnson elected House speaker with unanimous GOP support, ending weeks of chaos," CBS News, October 25, 2023, https://www.cbsnews.com/live-updates/house-speaker-vote-live-updates-10-25-2023/.

101 Matt Lavietes, "New House speaker's views on LGBTQ issues come under fresh scrutiny," NBC News, October 26, 2023, https://www.nbcnews.com/nbc-out/out-politics-and-policy/mike-johnson-house-speaker-lgbtq-views-scrutiny-rcna122317.

NOTES

102 Tal Axelrod, "Mike Johnson helped lead efforts to overturn the 2020 election. What that could mean for 2024," ABC News, October 27, 2023, https://abcnews.go.com/Politics/mike-johnson-led-efforts-overturn-2020-election-2024/story?id=104351307.

103 U.S. Congressman Mike Johnson, "Committees and Caucuses," accessed July 17, 2024, https://mikejohnson.house.gov/about/committees-and-caucuses.htm.

104 U.S. Congressman Mike Johnson, "In the News," accessed July 17, 2024, https://mikejohnson.house.gov/news/documentsingle.aspx?DocumentID=1267.

105 Lawrence v. Texas, 539 U.S. 558 (2003), Justia, U.S. Supreme Court, accessed February 14, 2024, https://supreme.justia.com/cases/federal/us/539/558/.

106 Gallup, "Islamophobia: Understanding Anti-Muslim Sentiment in the West," Gallup, World, accessed July 17, 2024, https://news.gallup.com/poll/157082/islamophobia-understanding-anti-muslim-sentiment-west.aspx.

107 The Associated Press, "Mahsa Amini, the Kurdish-Iranian woman who died in police custody, is awarded EU human rights prize," AP, last updated October 19, 2023, https://apnews.com/article/eu-sakharov-prize-masha-amini-5a24ba82e8b7819afae72e9dff4bc25e.

108 ABC News, "North Carolina's 'bathroom bill' replacement goes to governor," ABC News, March 30, 2017, https://abcnews.go.com/Politics/north-carolinas-bathroom-bill-replacement-now-governor/story?id=46465388#:~:text=The%20proposed%20bill%20passed%20in%20the%20state%20legislature%20today.

109 Mark Joseph Stern, "The Real Reason the Religious Right Opposes Trans Equality," Slate, May 4, 2016, https://slate.com/human-interest/2016/05/trans-bathroom-predator-myth-is-rooted-in-religion.html.

110 Marcie Bianco, "Statistics Show Exactly How Many Times Trans People Have Attacked You in Bathrooms," MIC, April 2, 2015, https://www.mic.com/articles/114066/statistics-show-exactly-how-many-times-trans-people-have-attacked-you-in-bathrooms.

111 Dictionary.com, s.v. "ignorance (*n.*)," accessed February 14, 2024, https://www.dictionary.com/browse/ignorance.

112 *Merriam-Webster.com Dictionary*, s.v. "stupid (*a.*)," accessed January 17, 2024, https://www.merriam-webster.com/dictionary/stupid.

113 Dictionary.com, s.v. "fascism (*n.*)," accessed January 17, 2024, https://www.dictionary.com/browse/fascism.

114 Matthew Spalding, "The Man Who Would Not Be King," The Heritage Foundation, February 5, 2007, https://www.heritage.org/commentary/the-man-who-would-not-be-king.

NOTES

115 Dictionary.com, s.v. "fact (*n.*)," "fiction (*n.*)," accessed January 17, 2024, https://www.dictionary.com/browse/fact, https://www.dictionary.com/browse/fiction, https://www.dictionary.com/browse/fiction.

116 Ozan Varol, "Facts Don't Change People's Minds. Here's What Does," Next Big Idea Club, September 8, 2017, https://nextbigideaclub.com/magazine/facts-dont-change-peoples-minds-heres/16242/.

117 Bible Study Tools, Matthew 7:2, King James Version, accessed February 14, 2024, https://www.biblestudytools.com/kjv/matthew/7-2.html.

118 Bible Study Tools, John 13:5, King James Version, accessed February 14, 2024, https://www.biblestudytools.com/kjv/john/13-5.html.

119 Collinsdictionary.com, s.v. "faith (*n.*)," accessed January 17, 2024, https://www.collinsdictionary.com/dictionary/english/faith.

120 American Medical Association, "Sexual orientation and gender identity change efforts (so-called 'conversion therapy')," AMA, accessed January 17, 2024, https://www.ama-assn.org/system/files/conversion-therapy-issue-brief.pdf.

121 Robin Opsahl, "Trump at Iowa event says Jan. 6 participants acted 'patriotically and peacefully,'" Iowa Capital Dispatch, January 6, 2024, https://iowacapitaldispatch.com/2024/01/06/trump-at-iowa-event-says-jan-6-participants-acted-patriotically-and-peacefully/.

122 Republican National Convention, "Republic Platform 2016," RNC 2016 Cleveland, 2016, https://prod-cdn-static.gop.com/media/documents/DRAFT_12_FINAL%5B1%5D-ben_1468872234.pdf.

123 Dictionary.com, s.v. "traitor (*n.*)," accessed January 17, 2024, https://www.dictionary.com/browse/traitor.

124 Brian Naylor, "Read Trump's Jan. 6 Speech, A Key Part of Impeachment Trial," NPR, February 10, 2021, https://www.npr.org/2021/02/10/966396848/read-trumps-jan-6-speech-a-key-part-of-impeachment-trial.

125 U.S. Congress, *United States Code: Riots, 18 U.S.C. §§ -2102 (Suppl. 5, 1964),* Library of Congress, accessed January 17, 2024, https://www.loc.gov/item/uscode1964-023018102/.

126 Brandenburg v. Ohio, 395 U.S. 444 (1969), Justia, U.S. Supreme Court, accessed January 17, 2024, https://supreme.justia.com/cases/federal/us/395/444/.

127 Steve Hollier, "What do Wesley Snipes and Al Capone Have in Common?" Wordpress, December 9, 2010, https://stevehollier.wordpress.com/2010/12/09/what-do-wesley-snipes-and-al-capone-have-in-common/.

NOTES

128 Jeff Wagner, "What is the RICO Act, and how does it impact organized crime?" CBS News, August 22, 2023, https://www.cbsnews.com/minnesota/news/rico-act-explainer/.

129 Hymes, Clare, "Trump faces a RICO charge in Georgia. What is the Racketeer Influenced and Corrupt Organizations Act?" CBS News, last updated August 15, 2023, https://www.cbsnews.com/news/trump-georgia-indictment-what-are-rico-charges/.

130 Barton Gellman, "Iraq's Family Feud Leaves Bloody Trail," *The Washington Post*, February 10, 1997, https://www.washingtonpost.com/archive/politics/1997/02/10/iraqs-family-feud-leaves-bloody-trail/ed574d7e-a1b8-4fac-8034-3adda7d125f9/.

131 Rob Garver, "Trump Celebrates Jan. 6 Attack in Large Campaign Rally," VOA News, March 27, 2023, https://www.voanews.com/a/trump-celebrates-jan-6-attack-in-large-campaign-rally/7024839.html.

132 Carroll v. Trump, 498 F. Supp. 3d 422 (S.D.N.Y. 2020), https://casetext.com/case/carroll-v-trump-2.

133 Carrie Johnson, "DOJ won't shield Trump from claims he defamed writer E. Jean Carroll," NPR, July 11, 2023, https://www.npr.org/2023/07/11/1187100364/trump-carroll-lawsuit.

134 Kaela Malig, "A Guide to the Criminal Cases Against Donald Trump," PBS, January 30, 2024, https://www.pbs.org/wgbh/frontline/article/a-guide-to-the-criminal-cases-against-donald-trump/.

135 The Federal Bureau of Investigation, "Al-Qaeda International," FBI, accessed January 17, 2024, https://archives.fbi.gov/archives/news/testimony/al-qaeda-international.

136 Department of Homeland Security, "MYTH/FACT: Known and Suspected Terrorists/Special Interest Aliens," DHS, released January 7, 2019, https://www.dhs.gov/news/2019/01/07/mythfact-known-and-suspected-terroristsspecial-interest-aliens.

137 Cynthia Vinney, "What is a Cult of Personality?" Verywell Mind, October 1, 2021, https://www.verywellmind.com/what-is-a-cult-of-personality-5191337.

138 Candice Lucey, "What Is the Mark of the Beast in the Bible?" Christianity.com, last updated December 28, 2023, https://www.christianity.com/wiki/end-times/what-is-the-mark-of-the-beast-in-the-bible.html.

139 Anthony Izaguirre and Brendon Farrington, "Florida expands 'Don't Say Gay'; House OKs anti-LGBTQ bills," AP, April 19, 2023, https://apnews.com/article/desantis-florida-dont-say-gay-ban-684ed25a303f83208a89c556543183cb.

140 Abigail McLeod, "I'm a Teacher in Florida. The Anti-LGBTQ Rules Are Making the Job Nearly Impossible." Slate, October 28, 2022, https://slate.com/news-and-politics/2022/10/florida-teacher-takedown-ron-desantis-dont-say-gay-bill.html.

NOTES

141 Catherine E. Shoichet, "Undocumented immigrants are paying their taxes today, too," CNN, last updated April 18, 2023, https://www.cnn.com/2023/04/18/us/undocumented-immigrants-taxes-cec/index.html.

142 Joe Carter, "Evangelical and LGBT+ Ally: Why You Can't Be Both," The Gospel Coalition, August 29, 2022, https://www.thegospelcoalition.org/article/evangelical-lgbt-ally/.

143 Tom Gjelten, "Peaceful Protesters Tear-Gassed To Clear Way For Trump Church Photo-Op," NPR, June 1, 2020, https://www.npr.org/2020/06/01/867532070/trumps-unannounced-church-visit-angers-church-officials.

144 Will Rahn and Dan Patterson, "What is the QAnon conspiracy theory?" CBS News, last updated March 29, 2021, https://www.cbsnews.com/news/what-is-the-qanon-conspiracy-theory/.

145 Chris Cillizza, "What is 'Trump Derangement Syndrome' – and do you have it?" CNN, July 20, 2018, https://www.cnn.com/2018/07/19/politics/trump-derangement-syndrome/index.html.

146 Melissa Block, "The clear and present danger of Trump's enduring 'Big Lie,'" NPR, December 23, 2021, https://www.npr.org/2021/12/23/1065277246/trump-big-lie-jan-6-election.

147 Hope Yen, "AP FACT CHECK: Yes, Trump lost election despite what he says," AP, May 6, 2021, https://apnews.com/article/donald-trump-michael-pence-electoral-college-elections-health-2d9bd47a8bd3561682ac46c6b3873a10.

148 Emilie Lehmann-Jacobsen, "How to Control the Masses by Silencing the Press," *The Diplomat*, January 15, 2021, https://thediplomat.com/2021/01/how-to-control-the-masses-by-silencing-the-press/.

149 Michael M. Grynbaum, "Trump Calls the News Media the 'Enemy of the American People,'" *The New York Times*, February 17, 2017, https://www.nytimes.com/2017/02/17/business/trump-calls-the-news-media-the-enemy-of-the-people.html.

150 Brett Samuels, "Trump ramps up rhetoric on media, calls press 'the enemy of the people,'" The Hill, April 5, 2019, https://thehill.com/homenews/administration/437610-trump-calls-press-the-enemy-of-the-people/.

151 Kent v. Dulles, 357 U.S. 116 (1958), Justia, https://supreme.justia.com/cases/federal/us/357/116/.

152 Claire Hansen, Horus Alas, and Elliott Davis Jr., "Where Is Marijuana Legal? A Guide to Marijuana Legalization," *U.S. News*, November 8, 2023, https://www.usnews.com/news/best-states/articles/where-is-marijuana-legal-a-guide-to-marijuana-legalization.

NOTES

153 Planned Parenthood Action Fund, "Is Abortion Still Accessible in My State Now That Roe v. Wade Was Overturned?" Planned Parenthood, accessed January 17, 2024, https://www.plannedparenthoodaction.org/abortion-access-tool/US.

154 Jonathan Landay and Simon Lewis, "US intelligence report alleging Russia election interference shared with 100 countries," Reuters, October 20, 2023, https://www.reuters.com/world/us/us-intelligence-report-alleging-russia-election-interference-shared-with-100-2023-10-20/.

155 Philip Bump, "Figuring out how many 'MAGA Republicans' there actually are," *The Washington Post*, September 2, 2022, https://www.washingtonpost.com/politics/2022/09/02/trump-republicans-biden-maga/.

156 Marshall Cohen, Morayo Ogunbayo, and Nick Valencia, "Trump attorney Sidney Powell pleads guilty in Georgia election subversion case," CNN, October 20, 2023, https://www.cnn.com/2023/10/19/politics/sidney-powell-fulton-county-georgia-2020-election-subversion/index.html.

157 Mac Brower, "What's Next in Republicans' Legal War on Voting Rights," Democracy Docket, July 27, 2023, https://www.democracydocket.com/analysis/whats-next-in-republicans-legal-war-on-voting-rights/.

GRATITUDE

I WANTED TO TAKE THE TIME TO THANK everyone who helped me make this book a reality. To protect the brave souls who helped me with this book and its message, I have not included their names. You know who you are.

First, to those close to me. Thank you for believing in me and supporting me throughout the process of publishing a book. Not just the long hours of writing it, but all the other things we had to do to make this happen.

To a new friend, and published author, thank you for taking the time to help a new writer.

To my editor and fact-checker, graphic designer, mentors, publisher, publicist, lawyers, and development coaches, thank you. Again, this book would never have existed anywhere but on my computer if it weren't for all of you.

To my beta readers. Without your invaluable feedback this book wouldn't be as good, or as polished, as it is. My first draft, all the way through to the final draft, couldn't have been done without you.

To the agents I worked with, some for over twenty years, thank you. Many of you were MAGA, and without your "Owning the Libs" moments, I would not have had such good information for my book. You have given me much-needed insight into the thinking and behavior of MAGA in our government. To the agents who spoke up against MAGA, or even who were quietly anti-MAGA, thank you!

To all true Americans, both civilians and government employees, who are fighting against MAGA, thank you for your continued effort to save our country from MAGA and Trump.

And especially to you, my reader. I appreciate your support but, even more importantly, I appreciate your interest in protecting our country from tyranny. Thank you.

May you always be free.

ABOUT THE AUTHOR

RUSSELL K. JACK is a retired US senior federal air marshal and a first-time author. He hopes this book will promote critical thinking about protecting our democracy and just how precariously close we are to losing it forever. He writes this book out of a sense of duty to the American people. There will be many who express views for, and against, what he has written. Let us hope that they can stick to factual information for their dialogue, and not just use worn-out tropes from talking heads, and easily disproven misinformation.

   Russell wrote this book not just as a catharsis for his struggles with patriotism versus the MAGA movement, but also as a handy guide to answering a debate with any MAGA supporter. Now you can say to them, "Just read the book."

www.ingramcontent.com/pod-product-compliance
Lightning Source LLC
Chambersburg PA
CBHW020543030426
42337CB00013B/955